Letter Writing —— in —— German

A. Baveja

Head of German
St. Joseph's School, Workington, Cumbria

—— Bell & Hyman ——

First published in 1985 by
Bell & Hyman Limited
Denmark House
37–39 Queen Elizabeth Street
London SE1 2QB

British Library Cataloguing in Publication Data
Baveja, A.
    Letter writing in German.
    1. Letter-writing, German—Examinations,
    questions, etc.
    I. Title
    808.6   PF3483

    ISBN 0-7135-2459-6

Phototypeset in 10/11 Garamond ITC by
Tradespools Ltd, Frome, Somerset
Produced in Great Britain by
M & A Thomson Litho Limited, East Kilbride

For
my parents
and
Carlota Wentzel

A word in one language seldom answers entirely to any single word in another, so that what are called synonyms are really only approximately such ...

Elizabeth Weir
Preface to *Cassell's New German Dictionary*, 1889

Preface

This book has been prepared with the needs of candidates for all public examinations in German in mind, but it should be especially useful to those taking school examinations such as CSE, SCE, GCE 'O' or 'A' Level and the proposed GCSE. A comprehensive guide to writing letters in German, incorporating the very latest trends, has been included. This should be of particular interest to those studying German on their own or at evening classes. It should be emphasised, however, that this book is not intended to be a guide to writing commercial correspondence, which is beyond the scope of this work.

The majority of the model letters in this book are edited versions of authentic letters. They include a range of modern colloquial expressions, which often escape the attention of teachers.

I have attempted to arrange the units in order of difficulty, but it would be presumptuous on my part to expect any teacher to tackle the units in the order in which they are presented. However, they may find my grading efforts helpful.

Each model letter is followed by comprehension exercises. Exercise A should be beneficial for all pupils. Exercise B has been carefully planned to elicit natural responses or full answers from the learner, whether written or oral. As the various examination boards have different policies regarding comprehension and manipulation exercises, teachers may wish to adapt Exercise B to suit their particular needs. Exercise C should be of general use. The questions encourage the learner to use the first person singular and plural, the two most common verb forms used in writing letters.

Each unit also contains either a cloze-type exercise or a translation in the form of a letter. In my experience these are the two most rewarding types of exercises to prepare candidates for the letter writing part of public examinations. The teacher should regard these exercises, particularly the translation, as a means towards an end, two useful tools for practice in writing letters in a foreign language. Seen in this context the translation should make sense to those teachers who frown upon translations as old-fashioned and/or unproductive. I would agree with them that a translation, practised as an isolated exercise without any relevance to a real life situation, has very limited value.

The cloze-type exercise and the translation could be treated as follows, though individual teachers may prefer a different approach:

Stage 1: This should involve the whole class, with the learner providing oral responses in German to the printed stimuli in the cloze exercise or translation.

Stage 2: Pupils should be required to produce a written version of the letter as a cloze exercise or translation, either in class or as homework.

Stage 3: The teacher may wish to correct each piece of work individually. Alternatively, the work could be assessed collectively in class, to the benefit of all pupils.

Stage 4: The teacher should ask pupils to provide the correct responses orally. The correct version could be written on the blackboard and the pupils asked to copy this version in a separate exercise book for such model letters and allied material. All too often nowadays the blackboard is neglected by teachers, and pupils do not see the final fair versions of such exercises, with the result that they cannot put to paper what they have often heard in the classroom but perhaps have never seen in writing.

Ideally, the vocabulary in each unit should be mastered by the class before proceeding to Exercise F or the next unit, as the case may be. Exercise F, a consolidation test, where the learner is expected to write a letter on a subject related to the matter in the unit, can be done as a class activity or as a piece of individual work, depending on the strengths and weaknesses of the class as a whole.

A comprehensive glossary, containing stock phrases and idiomatic expressions relating to the units in this book, is provided for use with the relevant topics. As an examiner, I feel teachers and pupils will find this an additional aid to writing letters in German.

In addition to all those whose correspondence I have used, edited or mutilated to produce this book I would like to offer my thanks to the following for their suggestions and practical help: Allan Spargo; Bernard Sweeney; Martin Parnell, William C. Mitchell and the production team at Bell & Hyman.

In conclusion, I would like to thank Werner F. Vogt of Bremen for his invaluable advice regarding the presentation of material in this book, which would not have been completed without his help.

A.B.
Maryport and Bremen, 1985

Contents

Guidelines

Section A. Informal letters

1. Address and date

Generally Germans write only the name of their home town followed by the date, on the top right-hand side of the writing paper. Neither the full address nor the year is written as a rule, e.g. *Hamburg, den 14. Februar*.

This is the most popular form for writing the date, but there are others. The most common are:

Hamburg, den 14. Februar 1984
Hamburg, den 14. Februar 84
Hamburg, den 14.2.1984
Hamburg, den 14.02.1984
Hamburg, d. 14.2.84
Hamburg, 14.2.84

In English the date may begin with the day, e.g. '14th February', or it may begin with the month, e.g. 'February 14th'. In German the date must *always* begin with the day. No exceptions!

The sender's address is normally written on the envelope, either in the top left-hand corner or on the reverse. Occasionally, when a letter is being written to a particular person for the first time, it may be written above the date on the writing paper, as in English, in which case the date is written as follows:

Haffkruger Weg 35
2000 Hamburg 73

den 14. Februar

2. Salutation

In English we normally begin both formal and informal letters with the word 'Dear', e.g. 'Dear Richard', 'Dear Louise' or 'Dear Mr Benison'. This part of the letter is called the salutation. In German there are several ways of saying 'Dear', depending on whether we are writing an informal or a formal letter.

Informal letters are those written to:

Friends (including acquaintances) =   F
Relations   =   R
Young people   =   Y

with whom we are on *first-name terms*, and whom we address with the informal *du* in German. In this book we shall call this group of people FRY from now on.

In English we always finish a salutation with a comma, e.g. 'Dear Richard,' or 'Dear Louise,'. In German the salutation normally finishes with an exclamation mark, e.g. *Lieber Richard!* or *Liebe*

Louise! This is the traditional way to write the salutation in German.

Some people prefer to put a comma after the salutation instead of an exclamation mark. In such cases the first word in the first paragraph must always begin with a small letter, in both formal and informal letters. This kind of salutation is used in the model letters in Units 6, 7, 12 and 16.

Male FRY: When writing in German to male FRY we usually begin a letter with *Lieber*, e.g.:

Lieber Richard!   *Lieber Hans!*   *Lieber Onkel.*
Lieber Onkel Max!   *Lieber Vater!* (or *Lieber Vati!*)

Female FRY: When writing in German to female FRY we begin a letter with *Liebe*, e.g.:

Liebe Louise!   *Liebe Ursula!*   *Liebe Tante!*
Liebe Tante Barbara!   *Liebe Mutter!* (or *Liebe Mutti!*)

Neuter FRY: Occasionally we may want to write a letter to someone very close to us, for whom we have a term of endearment. In German, such words of endearment usually end in *-chen* or *-lein*, e.g. *Paulchen* or *Ingelein*. Since all words ending in *-chen* and *-lein* are neuter nouns, we use the neuter *Liebes* with such names, e.g. *Liebes Paulchen!* or *Liebes Ingelein!* It does not matter whether we are writing to a male (e.g. Paul) or a female (e.g. Inge).

The same goes for letters to someone whose title is 'Miss': here the salutation is, for example, *Liebes Fräulein Armstrong!* since *Fräulein* is a neuter noun. Letters with this salutation are formal—formal letters are explained in Section B.

(Similarly, if we are writing a letter to a person without using his or her name, e.g. *Kind* or *Mädchen*, we use the neuter *Liebes* to address them, e.g. *Liebes Kind!* or *Liebes Mädchen!* since these too are neuter nouns.)

Plural FRY: If we are writing to two or more FRY, we address them individually, with *Lieber* or *Liebe* (or *Liebes*), but with only one exclamation mark at the end of the salutation:

Lieber Vater, lieber Onkel!
Liebe Louise, liebe Barbara!
Lieber Richard, lieber Max, lieber Paul!

Where we are writing to both male and female FRY, we must always address the female(s) first, with *Liebe*, followed by the male(s), with *lieber:*

Liebe Mutti, lieber Vati!
Liebe Louise, liebe Barbara, lieber Richard!

With neuter FRY, the 'ladies first' rule still applies, e.g.:

Liebes Ingelein, liebes Paulchen!

If we are writing to grown-ups (FRY) and children (FRY) they will normally all be relatives. The grown-ups always come first (ladies first) and the youngest person or neuter FRY usually comes last, e.g.:

Liebe Tante Doris, lieber Onkel Alfred, liebe Ina, liebes Karlchen!

Liebe Mutti, lieber Vati, liebe Louise, liebes Ingelein!
Liebe Eltern, lieber Paul, liebes Ingelein!
but *Liebe Eltern, liebes Ingelein, liebes Paulchen!* (ladies first)
Most people prefer to use collective nouns to address a group of friends or other people, e.g. 'Dear Friends,' 'Dear Members,' 'Dear Parents,'. In such cases we use the plural *Liebe* to begin our salutation, e.g.:

Liebe Freunde!   *Liebe Mitglieder!*
Liebe Eltern!   *Liebe Kameraden!*

(If we wish to say 'My dear friends', the equivalent German form would be: *Meine lieben Freunde!* etc. (*lieben* = plural adjective after *Meine*.)

NOTE: Many young people nowadays have adopted the salutation *Hallo!* in letters to FRY, e.g.

Hallo Richard!   *Hallo Freunde!*
Hallo Louise!   *Hallo Klassenkameraden!*

It is advisable *not* to use this form of salutation in an examination.

3. Body of the letter

(a) The salutation should normally be followed by a blank line and the first word of the first paragraph must always begin under the first letter of the salutation, no matter which type of salutation we choose or what kind of letter we are writing. This is the traditional way to begin the letter. There is no indenting for paragraphs in German: new paragraphs always start at the very beginning of the line.

(b) The person or persons we are writing to must be addressed with capital letters at all times when we use any forms of the following words:

	(Nom.)	(Acc.)	(Dat.)	(Your)
Singular:	Du	Dich	Dir	Dein
Plural:	Ihr	Euch	Euch	Euer

(c) Whenever possible try not to begin a paragraph or sentence with the word '*Ich*'. Avoiding it at the beginning of a sentence, particularly in letters where you are writing a lot about yourself, makes for better style and introduces variety.

(d) A letter does not necessarily have to be long to make it interesting, but you should always remember the following points:

If replying to a letter begin by acknowledging receipt of the letter and then answer any definite questions that may have been asked by the person you are writing to.

If replying to a specific invitation, e.g. for holidays, to a party or an outing, always repeat the date and time just in case there may have been an error in the letter you received. Remember to thank the person(s) for the invitation. However, the letter should not be over-formal if you are writing to FRY.

If writing a letter of thanks for a gift remember to try and be enthusiastic or appreciative. Similarly if you have been staying with someone your letter of thanks could mention all the things you particularly enjoyed during your stay.

4. Signing-off

There is no direct translation of such phrases as 'Yours sincerely,' 'Yours affectionately,' and so forth. You should try to finish an informal letter by choosing a phrase from the section headed 'Finishing a letter' in the Glossary of Stock Phrases at the end of this book, which gives you some of the more popular current ways of ending letters.

Instead of saying 'Yours sincerely' and 'Yours affectionately' etc., most Germans writing informal letters use the following terms:

A male writing a letter uses *Dein* (Yours) before signing off. A female uses *Deine*, e.g.

  Dein Richard   or *Deine Louise*

A male writing to two or more people uses *Euer* before signing off. A female uses *Eure*, e.g.

  Euer Richard   or *Eure Louise*

If two or more people are writing the letter the appropriate form is *Deine* if they are writing to one person and *Eure* if they are writing to two or more persons, e.g.

  (a) *Deine*   (b) *Eure*
   Louise und Richard   *Erika und Hermann*

If two or more people are writing the letter the female(s) should always sign first, as in the above examples.

5. Writing to a family

Letters written to a whole family usually take the salutation *Liebe Familie ...!* e.g. *Liebe Familie Schmidt!*

If we are on Christian-name terms with *all* the members of the family we are writing to, we can use the informal plural forms of address for FRY in the body of the letter, i.e. *Ihr, Euch, Euer* (see Section A, part 3).

If we are on Christian-name terms with only *some* members of the family, we should use the formal plural forms of address, i.e. *Sie, Ihnen, Ihr*, as for formal letters.

Section B. Formal letters

Formal letters are those we write to people with whom we are not on first-name terms. There are two types of formal letters:

 (i) Letters to people we address with *Sie*, i.e.:

  Grown-ups   =   G
  Acquaintances   =   A
  Strangers   =   S

We shall refer to this group of people as GAS.

 (ii) Business letters.

1. Address and date

The date and address in letters to GAS is usually written in exactly the same way as in letters to FRY. If writing to strangers for the first time, e.g. about an *au pair* situation or exchange programme for pupils or students, we may, if we wish to do so, write the address on the top right-hand side of the writing paper, though it is perfectly normal to write the address only on the envelope.

If we are writing a business letter, e.g. to a hotel, travel agency or company, we may write the address on either the top right-hand side of the writing paper or on the top left-hand side. It is usual to write the date in full in all business letters, e.g. *den 10.2.84* or *Bremen, den 15.6.1984*. It is important that we give the year as well, as business letters are normally filed away for future reference. As in English, the name and address of the addressee is written just above the salutation. (See the model letters in Units 14–17 for examples of business letters.)

2. Salutation

If we are writing to GAS we may choose one of the following salutations to begin the letter:

> *Sehr geehrter Herr Schmidt!* = Dear Mr Schmidt,
> *Sehr geehrte Frau Schmidt!* = Dear Mrs Schmidt,
> *Sehr geehrtes Fräulein* (or *Frl.*) *Schmidt!* = Dear Miss Schmidt,

Note: we write:

> *Sehr geehrter Herr Dr. Schmidt!* (never: *Sehr geehrter Dr. Schmidt!*)

or
> *Sehr geehrte Frau Dr. Schmidt!* (never: *Sehr geehrte Dr. Schmidt!*)

If we are writing to two or more people we must repeat the salutation for each person as in informal letters, e.g.

> *Sehr geehrter Herr Schmidt, sehr geehrter Herr Koenen!*

If we are writing to a female GAS and a male GAS the female must be addressed first and we may use the following variation in the form of salutation to introduce variety:

> *Sehr verehrte Frau Schmidt, sehr geehrter Herr Schmidt!*

If we know the people to whom we are writing quite well, but are not on Christian-name terms with them, we may use the following salutations which are slightly less formal:

> *Lieber Herr Schmidt!, Liebe Frau Schmidt!, Liebes Frl. Schmidt!*
> *Liebe Frau Schmidt, lieber Herr Schmidt!*
> *Lieber Herr Dr. Schmidt!, Liebe Frau Dr. Schmidt!*

If we are writing formal business letters we do not have to address the person(s) we are writing to by name. The following salutations are normally used in German business correspondence:

(a) *Sehr geehrte Herren!* = Dear Sirs,

This is by far the most common salutation in letters to hotels, firms, government offices and prospective employers.

(b) *Sehr geehrte Damen und Herren!* or *Meine sehr geehrten Damen und Herren!* = Dear Ladies and Gentlemen (Ladies first). This form is often used when writing to a firm e.g. of solicitors, where some of the solicitors are women, or writing to a firm in which your letter may be dealt with by men or women.

(c) *Sehr geehrter Herr!* = Dear Sir, or
   Sehr geehrte Dame! = Dear Madam,

This form is used when we know we are dealing with only one man or only one woman.

When writing very formal business letters in German it is customary, as in English, to state what the letter is about after the word *Betreff* (Regarding) or *Betr.* (Re:)—See Units 16 & 17.

When writing very formal letters to government offices, e.g. an employment agency, it is not necessary to write a salutation (see Unit 17).

3. Body of the letter

In formal letters of any kind we must address the person(s) we are writing to with the forms *Sie, Ihnen, Ihr*, for both singular and plural. Remember that these words are *always* written with a capital (whether in letters or not).

Remember that (as for informal letters) the first word of the first paragraph begins under the first letter of the salutation, and that every paragraph of the letter should begin at the left-hand end of the line (i.e. not be indented).

4. Signing-off

The following are the most popular subscriptions, i.e. ways of concluding formal letters; the approximate English equivalents are not direct translations.

(a) *Mit freundlichen Grüßen* = 'Yours sincerely,'

This form is used when writing to GAS and to hotels, guest houses and youth hostels or when placing orders for goods.

(b) *Hochachtungsvoll* = 'Yours faithfully,'

This is the traditional way of subscribing a formal business letter.

Nowadays more and more firms use *Mit freundlichen Grüßen*, which is less stuffy and more friendly. Government offices, however, continue to use *Hochachtungsvoll*. In the majority of cases, it is perfectly acceptable for the individual writing a formal business letter to use the subscription *Mit freundlichen Grüßen*, but it is better to use the more formal *Hochachtungsvoll* when writing a letter of complaint.

(c) *Mit vorzüglicher Hochachtung* = 'Yours (very) respectfully' or 'Yours (very) truly'.

This form is still used by many people when writing to government departments or solicitors and vice versa. Large companies also use this subscription to letters when placing or accepting substantial orders for goods.

(d) If writing to GAS we may add *Ihr* (for letters written by a male) before signing off, e.g.

> *Ihr*
>> *Heinrich Schroeder*

A female would write, e.g.:

> *Ihre*
>> *Louise Schmidt*

If we are writing a formal business letter there is no need to write *Ihr* or *Ihre*. We simply sign off after *Hochachtungsvoll* or *Mit freundlichen Grüßen* as in Units 14–17.

Section C. Addressing the envelope

From time to time the Deutsche Bundespost (West German Postal Authority) issues guidelines on how to address envelopes. The following is the latest form:

Ursula Graubner
Ostendorpstraße 16
2800 Bremen 1

Eilzustellung

Herrn
Friedrich Karl Barner
Henseweg 21d

2000 Hamburg 67

(a) The address of the sender is written in the top left-hand corner of the envelope. (Some people continue to write it at the back, which was preferred by the Bundespost in the past.)

(b) Any special postal remarks, e.g. *Eilzustellung* (Special or Express Delivery) in the above example, are written just above the name and address of the addressee.

(c) Notice that *Herrn* (accusative case) is used to say 'Mr'— *never* Herr—and that this is given a line of its own.

(d) The number of the house comes *after* the name of the street.

(e) A space, about a line deep, is left blank between the street address and the name of the town. (The address of the person receiving the letter is, in fact, written in exactly the same way on the envelope as on the writing paper in business letters—see Units 14–17. *Exception:* If the letter is going abroad the names of the town and the country are written in capital letters.)

(f) Some countries in Europe, including all the German-speaking ones, have come to an agreement about addressing envelopes. Instead of writing the name of the country the letter is going to, the postal authorities of these countries recommend the use of the international identification letter(s) used on cars travelling abroad. This precedes the post-code and town, e.g.:

Herrn	*Frau*
Konrad Schaefer	*Karin Frick*
Gehölzweg 20	*Sieveringerstraße 75*
D–2000 HAMBURG 70	*A–1190 WIEN*

(g) If the letter is going to some other country, the form below left is recommended. Notice that another space is left between the town to which the letter is going and the name of the country.

However, the international symbols have caught on so well that you should not be surprised to receive a letter addressed as on the right:

Mit Luftpost – By Airmail

Mr.	*Herrn*
S. Bee	*S. McGee*
52 Janedale Crescent	*15 Strathblaire Road*
WHITBY, ONTARIO L1N 6Z5	*Battersea*
KANADA	*GB–LONDON SW11 1RG*

The address of the sender is supposed to be written in the top left-hand corner of the envelope in all cases.

(h) The Deutsche Bundespost keeps reminding its customers to affix stamps in the top right-hand corner of the envelope. This facilitates the cancelling process by machines.

Unit 1

Mein Wellensittich heißt Freddie!

Emden, den 14. Oktober

Liebe Sheila!

Ich heiße Nina Berger, bin 15 Jahre alt und in der 9. Klasse. Mein Englischlehrer hat mir gesagt, daß Du eine deutsche Brieffreundin suchst und da bin ich!

Ich habe schwarzes Haar, grüne Augen und bin ziemlich klein für mein Alter—nur 1,60 m groß. Mit diesem Brief bekommst Du ein Foto von mir. Wie siehst Du aus? Hoffentlich schickst Du mir auch ein Bild von Dir.

Ich habe zwei Brüder, die älter sind als ich und eine jüngere Schwester. Meine Brüder heißen Karl und Reinhard. Meine Schwester, die zehn Jahre alt ist, heißt Monika. Sie ist sehr frech und geht mir manchmal auf die Nerven. Hast Du auch Geschwister und sind sie nett?

Meine Hobbys sind Schwimmen, Lesen und Radfahren. Ich fahre normalerweise mit dem Rad zur Schule. Wenn es regnet, fährt mein Vater mich hin. Wir haben einen großen Opel. Ich habe einen ganz süßen Wellensittich. Er heißt Freddie und fängt gerade an zu sprechen. Seine ersten Worte waren: Nadu—das heißt na du! Ich finde es toll, daß er schon redet, denn ich habe ihn erst seit drei Monaten. Was sind Deine Hobbys?

Mein Vater ist Schlachtermeister von Beruf und besitzt eine große Metzgerei in der Innenstadt. Meine Mutter hilft ihm bei der Arbeit. Sie haben tagsüber sehr viel zu tun und sind abends immer müde.

Hoffentlich schreibst Du mir bald einen langen Brief und vergiß bitte nicht, ein Foto von Dir beizulegen!

Bis bald. Herzliche Grüße

Deine

Nina

ziemlich	rather
frech	cheeky
geht mir auf die Nerven	gets on my nerves
normalerweise	normally
der Wellensittich	budgerigar
toll	great
der Schlachtermeister	butcher
tagsüber	during the day
beilegen	enclose

Übungen

A. Answer the following questions in English:

   1   Why did Nina write this letter to Sheila?
   2   Describe Nina.
   3   How many people are there in the Berger household?
   4   What does Nina think of her sister?
   5   What do her parents do for a living?
   6   What are her favourite pastimes?
   7   How does she usually get to school?
   8   What has Nina requested Sheila to do when she replies to her letter?

B. Beantworten Sie folgende Fragen:

   1   Wie alt ist Nina?
   2   Von wem hat sie Sheilas Adresse bekommen?
   3   Wieviele Schwestern hat sie?
   4   Was für einen Vogel hat sie zu Hause?
   5   Wie kommt sie zur Schule, wenn es regnet?
   6   Was ist ihr Vater von Beruf?
   7   Wo arbeitet ihre Mutter?
   8   In welchem Stadtteil liegt die Metzgerei ihres Vaters?
   9   Was soll Sheila machen, wenn sie an Nina schreibt?

C. Imagine you are Nina and answer the following questions in German:

   1   Wer hat dir Sheilas Adresse gegeben?
   2   Wie alt sind deine Brüder?
   3   Wie kommst du gewöhnlich zur Schule?
   4   Was für ein Geschäft hat dein Vater?
   5   Wer hilft ihm bei der Arbeit?
   6   Warum geht deine Schwester dir manchmal auf die Nerven?
   7   Warum sind deine Eltern immer müde, wenn sie abends von der Metzgerei nach Hause kommen?
   8   Was für einen Wagen habt ihr?
   9   Was sind deine Hobbys?

D. Complete the following letter to Nina by filling in the blanks with the information supplied in English after the blanks. Each blank must be filled in by one German word. Refer to Nina's original letter and the words and expressions in Section E to find the vocabulary you require.

Maryport, – – – (date)

– – (Dear Nina)!

– – (Many thanks) – – – (for your letter). Ich habe mich sehr darüber gefreut.

– – (I am called) Sheila Robinson – – – – – – (and am almost 15 years old). – – – – (I have brown hair) – – – (and grey eyes). – – – – – –, (I am also not very tall) – – (only 164 centimetres). – – – – (I have one brother) – – – (and one sister). – – – – – – (My brother is twelve years old) – – – (and is called George). – – – – – – – – (My sister is a year older than I am) – – – (and is called Linda).

– – – – – (We live in a semi-detached house) am Stadtrand von Maryport. – – – – – (Maryport is a small town) – – – – – (and has about ten thousand inhabitants). – – – (The town lies) – – (on the) Nordwestküste Englands. – – – – – – (We have a very large garden) – – – (with two apple trees) – – – (and all kinds of flowers). – – – – – (My father does the gardening) – – – – – (but my mother and I) – – – (help him sometimes) dabei.

– – –, (You would like to know) – – – – (what my hobbies are). – – –, (I like swimming), – – (play badminton) – – (and collect) – – – (stamps and picture postcards) aus aller Welt. – – – –? (Do you also collect something?)

– – – – – – (My compulsory subjects at school are) – – – (English and mathematics) – – – – (and my optional subjects are) –, –, –, – – – (German, French, Biology, History and Geography). – – – – (Geography is my favourite subject). – – – – – – –, (Which subjects do you have at school) – – – – – – (and do you also have a favourite subject?)

So, ich mache jetzt Schluß. Du bekommst – – – (a long letter) – – – – – (and a photograph of me).

Hoffentlich – – (you will write) mir – – (again soon).

Tschüß

Deine

Sheila

E. Make sure you learn the following words and expressions:

allerlei all kinds of	**der Einwohner** inhabitant
die Ansichtskarte picture postcard	**das Fach** subject
beilegen to enclose	**der Federball** badminton
besitzen to own or possess	**frech** cheeky, impudent
das Einfamilienhaus detached house	**sich freuen über** to be pleased about (+ acc.)

die **Gartenarbeit** gardening

das Hobby (die Hobbys) hobby, pastime

die Innenstadt town-centre, heart of the city

die Metzgerei the butcher's shop

das (er, es, sie) geht _mir_ auf die Nerven this gets on my nerves

die Küste coast

das Pflichtfach compulsory subject

reden to talk or speak

sammeln to collect

die Sammlung collection

der Schlachtermeister (Metzger) butcher

Schluß machen to end, finish, close

der Stadtrand outskirts or edge of town

am Stadtrand on the outskirts of the town

tagsüber during the day

toll great, fantastic, fabulous

Tschüß 'Bye

das Wahlfach optional subject, subect of choice

der Wellensittich budgerigar

die Welt the world

ziemlich rather, quite

das Zweifamilienhaus semi-detached house, two storey house or house designed for two families

F. Write an imaginary letter to a boy or girl in Germany, on the lines of the letters in this unit, giving as much information about yourself as you can.

Unit 2

Geburt

»Ostfriesland-
Personalausweis«

Die glücklichen Eltern:
Marion und Peter
Hofmayer

Der stolze Bruder:
Knut

Anschrift:
Hebbelstraße 7
2953 Rhauderfehn

Name: Hofmayer
Vorname: Klaas
Geburtsdatum: 9. 2. 1981,
                        13.40 Uhr
Geburtsort: Leer
Gewicht: 3960 Gramm
Größe: 54 cm

Unterschrift

Übungen

A. Answer the following questions in English:

1 What are Knut's parents called?
2 Where do the Hofmayers live?
3 What is the postal code for Rhauderfehn?
4 What is Knut's brother called?
5 When and where was he born?
6 At what time was he born?
7 How much did he weigh at birth?
8 What was his height at birth?

B. Beantworten Sie folgende Fragen:

1 Wie heißen Knuts Eltern?
2 In welcher Stadt wohnen die Hofmayers?
3 In welcher Straße wohnen sie?
4 Wie heißt das neugeborene Kind?
5 Wie heißt Knuts Bruder mit Vornamen?
6 Wie heißt er mit Nachnamen?
7 Wann wurde er geboren?
8 Um wieviel Uhr?
9 Wo ist er geboren?
10 Wieviel wog er bei der Geburt?
11 Wie groß war er bei der Geburt?

12   Auf wen ist Knut sehr stolz?

13   Welche Postleitzahl hat Rhauderfehn?

C. Imagine you are Knut. Refer to the card announcing the birth of Klaas, the notes in the margin and the words and expressions in Section D to find the vocabulary you require to translate the following letter to your cousin Andrea into German.

Rhauderfehn
16th February

Dear Andrea,

I have some good news for you. I have a baby brother now. He is called Klaas and was born on 9th February at 1.40 pm in Leer. He weighed 3960 grammes at birth and his height is 54 centimetres.

My parents are of course very happy and I am very proud of my brother. He is very cute and cuddly. He does not cry much but he sleeps a lot. He wakes up only when he is hungry.

I hope you are well! How are Uncle Heinrich and Aunt Birgitt? I shall write to you again soon when I have more time.

In the meantime all the best. Give my regards to your parents.

'Bye

Yours

Knut

some good news	**eine gute Nachricht**
baby brother	**Brüderchen**
(give the time using the 24 hour clock)	
at birth	**bei der Geburt**
of course	**natürlich**
very	*use:* **unheimlich**
proud of my …	**stolz auf meinen …**
cute	**niedlich**
cuddly	**knuddelig**
in the meantime	**inzwischen**
Give my regards to …	**Viele Grüße an … (+ acc.)**
'Bye,	*say:* **Tschüß**

D. Make sure you learn these words and expressions:

die Anschrift address
aufwachen to wake up
das Brüderchen baby brother, little brother
das Geburtsdatum date of birth
der Geburtsort place of birth
das Gewicht weight
glücklich sein be happy
die Größe height
er ist 50 cm groß his height is 50 cm
knuddelig cuddly
der Nachname/der Familienname surname, family name
die Nachricht news
neugeboren new-born

niedlich cute
die Postleitzahl (abbr: PLZ) Postal code for a town—this is always written before the name of the town. The number following the name of the town denotes the postal district within that town.
der Stolz pride
stolz sein auf (+ acc.) to be proud of
die Uhrzeit/die Zeit time
viele Grüße an … (+ acc.) give my regards to …
der Vorname first name
weinen to cry
wiegen to weigh

Unit 3

Hoffentlich geht das!

Bremen, den 13. Mai

Lieber Robert!

Heute abend habe ich mehrmals versucht, Dich telefonisch zu erreichen. Das Telefon gibt aber bei Dir nur immer ein Besetztzeichen. Ich weiß nicht, was das bedeutet! Ich werde aber weiterhin probieren. Falls ich Dich nicht erreichen kann: ich will Ende Juli nach England fahren und möchte gern bei Dir wohnen, um von dort aus—wie im letzten Jahr—einige Wanderausflüge zu machen. Du weißt, ich finde den Lake District unheimlich schön.

Leider ist es für mich nicht möglich, länger als bis zum 23. Juli zu bleiben. Am 5. Juli oder am 7. Juli möchte ich hier losfahren. Was sagst Du dazu? Hoffentlich geht das! Schreib mir bitte sofort, oder besser, ruf mich mal an. Nach 17 Uhr bin ich fast immer zu Hause.

Ansonsten habe ich sehr viel Arbeit. Es macht mir aber Spaß.

Alles Gute und bis bald.

Dein

Joachim

das Besetztzeichen engaged tone
probieren/versuchen to try
unheimlich very
leider I'm afraid/ unfortunately
länger als longer than
was sagst du dazu? what do you say (to that)?
hoffentlich geht das I hope this is possible
ansonsten otherwise
es macht mir Spaß I enjoy it

Übungen

A. Answer the following questions in English:

1 What did Joachim do before writing this letter?
2 Why did he decide to write the letter?
3 What did he want to ask Robert on the phone?
4 How does Joachim know that he will like it in the Lake District in England?
5 When would he like to leave for England?
6 What does he ask Robert to do when he gets the letter?
7 What did Joachim do on his previous visit to England?
8 What is the best time to catch Joachim at home?

B. Beantworten Sie folgende Fragen:

1 Wo wohnt Joachim?
2 Wann hat er diesen Brief geschrieben?

3 Was hatte er versucht, bevor er den Brief schrieb?
4 Warum konnte er Robert telefonisch nicht erreichen?
5 Was will er weiterhin probieren?
6 Was will Joachim in den Sommerferien machen?
7 Wann möchte er abreisen?
8 Was hat er im letzten Jahr gemacht?
9 Wo hat er gewohnt?
10 Was fand er besonders schön in England?

C. Imagine you are Joachim and answer the following questions in German:

1 Wo wohnen Sie?
2 Warum haben Sie diesen Brief geschrieben?
3 Was haben Sie heute mehrmals versucht, bevor Sie den Brief schrieben?
4 Warum konnten Sie Robert telefonisch nicht erreichen?
5 Was wollen Sie weiterhin probieren?
6 Was wollen Sie in den Sommerferien machen?
7 Wann möchten Sie abfahren?
8 Was haben Sie im letzten Jahr gemacht?
9 Wo haben Sie dort gewohnt?
10 Was macht Ihnen Spaß?

D. Translate the following letter into German. Refer to Joachim's original letter, the notes in the margins and the words and expressions in Section E to find the vocabulary you require.

[Place and Date]

Dear Werner,

This morning I tried to telephone you several times but you were not at home.

I would like to visit you in the summer holidays. I hope this is possible. I would like to leave on 1st August. However, I can't stay longer than two weeks. My aunt from America is coming on a visit on 18th August and I am supposed to be here when she arrives. So I must return on 15th August by the latest. What do you say? Is that all right?

What is there to do and see in Bremen? Isn't there a well-known art gallery in Bremen? I would find something like that very interesting.

Otherwise I am well. Please let me know soon whether I may come in August or not.

Meanwhile all the best

Yours,

Henry

However ... *say:* **Ich kann aber nicht ...**
on a visit **zu Besuch**
So I must ... *say:* **I must therefore ...**
by the latest **spätestens**
to be all right *use:* **klappen**
What is there to do? *say:* **What can one do?**
well-known **bekannt**
famous **berühmt**
art gallery **die Bildergalerie** *or* **die Kunsthalle**
something like that **so etwas**
let me know *use:* **schreib mir**
meanwhile **inzwischen**

E. Make sure you learn the following words and expressions:

alles Gute   all the best
ansonsten (*or* **sonst**)   otherwise
der Ausdruck   expression
bedeuten   to mean
bekannt   well-known
berühmt   famous
das Besetztzeichen   engaged tone
   (telephone)
sich freuen auf (+ acc.)   to look
   forward to
falls   in case
geht das?   is that all right, is that
   possible?
hoffentlich geht das!   I hope that is
   possible
hoffentlich klappt das!   I hope it will
   work out, be all right
inzwischen   in the meantime
leider   I'm afraid, unfortunately

mehrmals   several times
so etwas   something like that
der Spaß   fun
es macht mir Spaß   I enjoy doing it, I
   find it fun
spätestens   by the latest, at the latest
unheimlich   very
unterbringen   to accommodate, to put up
was sagst du dazu?   what do you say
   (to that)?
weiterhin ... arbeiten   continue to
   work etc.
zu Besuch   on a visit
zu diesem Zeitpunkt   at this/that time
das Wiedersehen   reunion
ein baldiges Wiedersehen   an early
   reunion or meeting
zurückfahren   return, travel back
zurückkehren   return, come/go back

F. Imagine you are Robert. Write a reply to Joachim's letter
saying you won't be able to put him up in July because your
aunt from America will be visting you at that time. Ask him
whether he would like to come later. Use as many of the
following expressions as you can in your letter:

**bekommen/erhalten — gut, daß Du rechtzeitig
geschrieben hast — es tut mir leid, aber ... —
es geht also nicht — vielleicht — Ende Juli/Anfang
August/Mitte September — hoffentlich geht das/klappt
das — ich freue mich auf ein baldiges Wiedersehen**

Unit 4

Es hat uns Spaß gemacht!

Berlin, den 7. Mai

Liebe Astrid!

Ich hoffe, es geht Dir gut. Mit diesem Brief möchte ich mich für den schicken Pullover bedanken. Er ist zwar etwas zu groß, aber das habe ich ganz gerne.

Jetzt möchte ich einige Worte über unsere vierzehntägige Klassenfahrt nach England schreiben. Ich glaube, es hat uns allen sehr viel Spaß gemacht, auch mal die englische Landschaft und die Menschen dort kennenzulernen. Die Tagesfahrten waren auch sehr interessant. Am besten jedoch fand ich die Schottlandreise. Edinburgh ist eine bildhübsche Stadt. Leider war die Zeit zu kurz, um sich alles genau anzusehen. Der Abschied von Euch fiel mir besonders schwer. Die englischen Schüler waren alle so freundlich und hilfsbereit.

Es war sehr nett von Deinen Eltern, mir so viele Geschenke zu geben. Meine Oma und meine Eltern finden, daß der englische Tee ausgezeichnet schmeckt. Gestern stand ein Bild von uns und ein Artikel von der Englandfahrt in unserer Zeitung. Möchtest Du diese Zeitung haben?

In der Schule schreiben wir schon wieder so viele Klassenarbeiten. Englisch ist jetzt mein Lieblingsfach. Stell Dir mal vor, ich habe in meiner Englischarbeit eine Eins gekriegt. Nun muß ich schließen und noch einmal vielen Dank für den Pullover.

Viele Grüße auch an Deine Eltern.

Tschüß

Deine

Elke

sich bedanken für express thanks for
es hat uns Spaß gemacht it was (great) fun
jedoch however
bildhübsch pretty as a picture, lovely
sich alles genau ansehen to have a close look at everything
der Abschied parting, farewell
es fiel mir sehr schwer I found it very difficult
Klassenarbeiten written class tests
Stell dir mal vor just imagine
eine Eins grade one (A)

Übungen

A. Answer the following questions in English:

1 What kind of pullovers does Elke like wearing?
2 With whom did she go to England?
3 How long did she stay there?
4 What did she find very interesting?
5 What did she enjoy most of all?
6 Why does she mention tea in her letter?
7 Why does she offer to send Astrid the local newspaper?
8 What did she think of the English pupils?
9 Where would she have liked to spend some more time?
10 Why is it a busy time for her in school?

B. Beantworten Sie folgende Fragen:

1 Wofür möchte sich Elke bei Astrid bedanken?
2 Was für Pullover trägt sie besonders gern?
3 Mit wem fuhr sie nach Großbritannien?
4 Was hat ihr in England sehr viel Spaß gemacht?
5 Was gefiel ihr am meisten?
6 Wo wollte sie etwas länger bleiben?
7 Wie empfand sie den Abschied von den englischen Schülern?
8 Wie fand ihre Oma den Tee, den sie von Astrids Eltern bekam?
9 An welchem Tag stand ein Artikel über die Englandreise in der Zeitung, wo Elke wohnt?
10 Warum hat sie jetzt so viel zu tun?

C. Imagine you are Elke and answer the following questions:

1 Wofür möchtest du dich bei Astrid bedanken?
2 Welche Pullover trägst du gern?
3 Was konntest du in England kennenlernen?
4 Was für eine Stadt ist Edinburgh?
5 Wozu war die Zeit in Edinburgh zu kurz?
6 Wie war für dich der Abschied von den englischen Schülern?
7 Wie finden deine Eltern den englischen Tee?
8 In welcher Zeitung stand der Artikel über eure Englandfahrt?
9 Warum hast du jetzt so viel zu tun?
10 Welches ist nun dein Lieblingsfach?

D. Complete the following letter to Petra by filling in the blanks with the information supplied in English after the blanks. Each blank must be filled in by one German word. Refer to Elke's original letter and the words and expressions in Section E to find the vocabulary you require.

Carlisle, – – – [date]

– (Dear) Petra!

Wir sind – (yesterday) heil – – (at home) angekommen. – – – –
– (I found it very difficult) von – (you) Abschied zu nehmen,
denn – – (the time) bei Euch war – – (so interesting). – – (I
would like) mich auch – – – – (for the smart skirt) bedanken.

Ich –, (find) Hamburg ist – (really) – – – – (a very nice city). – –
(The people) sind so aufmerksam und – (helpful). Am – (best of
all) fand ich die Hafenrundfahrt. Auch der – (walk) in der
Innenstadt – (liked) mir sehr. – (Afterwards) war ich –
(naturally) – – (very tired).

– (Now) bin ich – (however) wieder zu Hause. Die – –
(fortnight) sind – (gone) und ich muß – (again) – (hard)
arbeiten. Mein – (favourite subject) – – – (in school) ist jetzt
Deutsch. – (Perhaps) kannst Du – (me) – – (next year) besser –
(understand). Kommst Du – – (in August) – – (to England)?
Meine Eltern sagen, Du kannst – – (with us) wohnen.

– (Once again) herzlichen – (thanks) für die – (fabulous) Zeit
bei Euch und – – – (write again soon).

– (Yours)

Lisa

E. Make sure you learn the following words and expressions:

der Abschied parting, farewell	**die Innenstadt** town centre, heart of
sich alles (genau) ansehen to have a	the city
(good) look at everything	**jedoch** however
aufmerksam sein to be considerate	**die Klassenarbeit** written class-test
sich (bei jm.) bedanken für to	**kriegen** to obtain, get
express thanks for, to thank someone	**das Lieblingsfach** favourite subject
for	**nachher** afterwards
bildhübsch as pretty as a picture	**noch einmal/nochmals** once more,
es hat uns Spaß gemacht we enjoyed	once again
it, it was fun	**der Rock** skirt
fabelhaft fabulous	**die Rundfahrt** round trip
das Fach subject	**schick** smart, chic
freundlich friendly	**spazierengehen** to go for a walk
gefallen (+ dat.) to like, enjoy	**der Spaziergang** walk
gern(e) haben to like	**vorbei** over, past
der Hafen harbour, port	**sich vorstellen** to imagine
heil safe, safely	**stell dir mal vor** just imagine
hilfsbereit helpful	**zwar** admittedly, 'granted', to be sure

F. Write a reply to Elke's original letter using as many of the
words and expressions in this unit as you can. Say what you
have been doing in school lately and ask her to send you the
newspaper she mentions in her letter.

Verlobung

Engagement card: traditional form

Die Verlobung meiner Tochter
Barbara Christina mit
Herrn Horst Detlev Hamann
gebe ich bekannt.

Carlota Wentzel
geb. Reichmann

2 Hamburg 13, Hochallee 109

Empfang am Sonnabend, dem 25. Mai,
in der Hochallee 109, 15 – 17 Uhr.

Meine Verlobung mit Fräulein
Barbara Christina Wentzel,
Tochter des verstorbenen Herrn
Carl Hermann Wentzel und
seiner Frau Carlota, geb. Reichmann,
freue ich mich anzuzeigen.

Horst Detlev Hamann

2 Hamburg 20, Husumer Straße 37

Mai 1985

Engagement card: contemporary form

Wir haben uns verlobt

Barbara Wentzel
Detlev Hamann
25. Mai 1985

2 Hamburg 13
Hochallee 109

2 Hamburg 20
Husumer Straße 37

Übungen

A. Answer the following questions in English:

1 Whose daughter has got engaged?
2 What is her fiancé's name?
3 When did the reception take place?
4 Where did it take place?
5 At what time did it start?
6 How long was it supposed to last?
7 What was Barbara's father called?
8 What was Frau Carlota Wentzel's name before she got married?

B. Beantworten Sie folgende Fragen:

1 Wessen Tochter hat sich verlobt?
2 Mit wem hat sie sich verlobt?
3 Bei wem wohnt Barbara?
4 Wo wohnen die Wentzels?
5 An welchem Tag fand der Empfang statt?
6 Zu welcher Zeit?
7 In welchem Stadtteil von Hamburg wohnt Barbaras Verlobter?
8 Wie hieß Barbaras Vater?

C. Imagine you are Barbara's sister Cornelia.
Complete the following letter to your friend Angelika, by filling in the blanks with the information supplied in English after the blanks. Each blank must be filled in by one word. Refer to Barbara's engagement card and the words and expressions in Section D to find the vocabulary you require.

Hamburg, – – (3rd May)

Notes

for a long time
   seit langem

as **als**

use 24-hour clock for
   times

at our place **bei uns**

– –! (Dear Angelika)

Wir haben – – – – – (not heard from each other for a long time). Na, – – – –? (How are you) Ich habe – – – – – (some wonderful news for you). – – – – – – – – (My sister Barbara is getting engaged on 25th May). Ich glaube, – – – – – (you know the young man). – – (He is called) – – – [give the name of Barbara's fiancé]. Barbara – – – – – – (and he were at the same school). – – – – – – (So they have known each other for years). Horst Detlev – – – – – (works as an engineer in Hamburg). – – – – – –, (He is very nice and friendly) – – – – – – (and he is very handsome). – – – – (He also has a sense of humour).

– – – – – – – – – – – – – – (The reception is taking place on 25th May between 3 and 5 pm at our house). – – – – (My mother and I) – – – –, (would be very pleased) – – – – (if you could come). – – –, (My mother says) – – – – –, (you can spend the night at our place). – – – – (What do you say to that)? Schreib mir bitte bald, – – – – (whether you can come)!

– – (All the best)

– (Yours)
Cornelia

22

D. Make sure you learn the following words and expressions:

als   as

anzeigen   to give notice of, announce

bei uns   at our place

bekanntgeben   to make public, announce

der Empfang   reception

gut aussehen   to be good looking

der Humor   sense of humour

Humor haben   have a sense of humour

der Ingenieur   engineer

kennen   to know

lange; seit langem   for a long time

die Nachricht   news

der Stadtteil   part of town, postal district

stattfinden   to take place

übernachten   to spend the night, stay overnight

der Verlobte   fiancé

die Verlobte   fiancée

die Verlobten   engaged couple

die Verlobung   engagement

Unit 6

Erst die Arbeit, dann das Vergnügen!

Hamburg, den 12. September

Liebe Andrea,

lange haben wir nichts voneinander gehört. Nun, solange die Adressen stimmen, können wir immer noch miteinander Kontakt aufnehmen.

Seit vier Monaten arbeite ich nicht mehr bei der Bundespost. Ich arbeite jetzt bei einer Firma, die Fahrräder exportiert. Die Arbeit gefällt mir sehr. Sie ist interessanter und ich verdiene viel mehr als früher. Ich bekomme nun fünf Wochen Urlaub im Jahr, eine Woche mehr als früher. Leider muß ich etwas früher aufstehen, weil die Firma am Stadtrand liegt, und die Busfahrt ungefähr eine Stunde dauert. Man kann nicht alles haben!

Und nun zu Dir. Ich möchte gerne wissen, wie es Dir geht, wo Du jetzt arbeitest und was Du machst. Gefällt Dir die Arbeit? Oder möchtest Du lieber woanders hin? Wo sind Deine Eltern jetzt? Und Deine Geschwister? So viele Fragen, aber vielleicht schreibst Du mal, oder Du kommst auch einmal nach Deutschland. Dann mußt Du mir ganz bestimmt rechtzeitig schreiben. Verstanden?

Bist Du manchmal in London? Ich fahre eventuell Mitte Februar nach London. Ich möchte dann eine Woche in der englischen Hauptstadt verbringen, aber das hängt von meinen Finanzen ab. Bis dahin muß ich fleißig arbeiten und sparen. Du weißt ja, erst die Arbeit, dann das Vergnügen!

Ich werde mich sehr freuen, wenn Du mir recht bald schreibst.

Mit herzlichen Grüßen

Deine

Silvia

stimmen	to be correct
Kontakt aufnehmen	to contact
bei der Post	at the post office
als früher	than before
man kann nicht alles haben	you can't have everything
mal/einmal	sometime
ganz bestimmt	most definitely
rechtzeitig	in good time
eventuell	possibly, perhaps
das hängt von ... ab	this depends on ...
erst die Arbeit, dann das Vergnügen	work before pleasure

Übungen

A. Answer the following questions in English:

1 Where does Silvia work?
2 What did she do before this?
3 When did she give up her previous job?
4 Why does she prefer her present job?
5 What does she not particularly like about her present job?
6 What must Andrea be sure to do if she decides to go to Germany?
7 What are Silvia's plans for February?
8 What will influence her decision?
9 What must she try to do if she really wants to go to London?

B. Beantworten Sie folgende Fragen:

1 Wo arbeitet Silvia?
2 Wann hat sie angefangen, bei dieser Firma zu arbeiten?
3 Wo hat sie früher gearbeitet?
4 Wo liegt die Exportfirma, bei der sie arbeitet?
5 Wie kommt Silvia dahin?
6 Warum gefällt ihr die neue Arbeit besser?
7 Was gefällt ihr nicht besonders?
8 Wieviel Urlaub bekommt sie im Jahr?
9 Wieviel Urlaub hat sie bei der Post bekommen?
10 Was sind ihre Pläne für Februar?

C. Imagine you are Silvia and answer the following questions in English:

1 Wann hast du diesen Brief geschrieben?
2 Wo wohnst du?
3 Wo arbeitest du jetzt?
4 Seit wann arbeitest du bei dieser Firma?
5 Wo hast du früher gearbeitet?
6 Wann hast du aufgehört, bei der Post zu arbeiten?
7 Wie fährst du zu deiner Arbeitsstelle?
8 Wie lange brauchst du dafür?
9 Warum gefällt dir die neue Arbeit besser?
10 Was gefällt dir nicht so sehr?
11 Wohin möchtest du im Februar fahren?

D. Translate the following letter into German. Refer to Silvia's letter to Andrea, the notes in the margins and the words and expressions in Section E to find the vocabulary you require.

Dear Sabine,

I have not heard from you for three months. What is the matter?
I hope you are not ill.

I am now working as a secretary in a school on the outskirts of
the town. The headmaster is very nice and the pupils are noisy
but friendly. I am still living at home.

Where are your parents now? Is your sister still at school? When
are you coming to England again? I would like to see you again
soon. My parents say you can stay with us when you are in
England. If you come in August we can visit my Aunt Louise in
the country. She has a large farm. The weather in August is
usually good. We can spend a few days there. I am sure you will
like it there. What do you say?

I hope to hear from you soon.

Yours

Carolyn

What is the matter? **Was ist los?**
as a secretary **als Sekretärin**
noisy *say:* **laut**
friendly **freundlich**
at home *say:* **bei meinen Eltern**
Is your sister still at school? *say:* **geht Deine Schwester noch zur Schule?**
with us **bei uns**
if/when **wenn**
in the country **auf dem Lande**
pure **rein**
sure **sicher**
you will like it there **es wird dir dort gefallen**

E. Make sure you learn the following words and expressions:

als Sekretärin arbeiten to work as a secretary
die Arbeitsstelle place of work
auf dem Lande in the country
bei einer Firma/der Post arbeiten/ usw. to work for a firm/at the post office/etc.
die Luft ist rein/frisch/sauber the air is pure/fresh/clean
erst die Arbeit, dann das Vergnügen first work, then pleasure/ work comes before play
ganz bestimmt most definitely
es gefällt mir (*from* **gefallen** + **dat.**) I like it
ich möchte lieber/viel lieber I would rather/much rather
immer noch/noch immer still
Kontakt aufnehmen mit make contact with
lange for a long time

laut loud, noisy, boisterous
man kann nicht alles haben you can't have everything
mehr als früher more than before
rechtzeitig in good time
der Schulleiter (*also* **Schuldirektor**) headmaster
sicher/ganz sicher sure/quite sure
der Stadtrand the outskirts of the town
am Stadtrand on the outskirts of the town
stimmen to be correct
es stimmt/das stimmt that is correct
der Urlaub holiday(s)
Urlaub bekommen/haben have a holiday
in Urlaub gehen to go on holiday
im Urlaub sein to be away on holiday
was ist los? what's the matter?, what's up?
zur Schule gehen to go to school

F. Imagine you are Andrea and write a reply to Silvia's original
letter. Use as many of the new words and expressions in this
unit as you can and make sure that you answer all her
questions.

Unit 7

Ein gesundes und glückliches Neues Jahr!

Wien, den 6. Januar

Lieber Philip,

ich habe mich sehr gefreut, von Dir zu hören. Vielen Dank auch für die hübsche Weihnachtskarte. Bitte entschuldige, daß ich erst heute schreibe, aber ich bin erst vor drei Tagen nach Hause zurückgekommen. Auch ich wünsche Dir ein gesundes und glückliches Neues Jahr.

Ski fahren	to go skiing
Schlittschuh fahren	to go (ice) skating
die Filiale	branch
Mensch!	gosh!
auf einen Haufen	all at once

Zu Weihnachten war ich zwei Wochen lang bei meinen Eltern in Kärnten. Wir hatten es sehr schön. Es gab viel Schnee und einen blauen Himmel, und wir konnten Ski und Schlittschuh fahren. Außerdem war mein Bruder aus Schweden auch da. Es war also ein richtiges Familienfest. Meine Eltern haben sich sehr darüber gefreut. Mein Bruder arbeitet als Koch in einem großen Hotel in Stockholm und kann normalerweise zu dieser Zeit nicht frei bekommen. Leider mußte ich als Erste wieder wegfahren.

Hier in Wien ist es nun grau und stürmisch. Als ich ankam und vom Bahnhof nach Hause fuhr, war es noch schlimmer. Ich arbeite nach wie vor in der Bank aber schon lange nicht mehr am Stephansplatz, sondern in einer Filiale bei der Oper. Die Arbeit macht mir Spaß.

Und wo warst Du zu Weihnachten? Auch bei Deinen Eltern? Habt Ihr etwas Besonderes gemacht? Was gab es dieses Jahr am ersten Weihnachtstag: Puter, Gans oder Ente? Hast Du wieder ein paar Pfund zugenommen? Sind Deine Weihnachtsferien zu Ende und arbeitest Du wieder? Mensch, so viele Fragen auf einen Haufen, aber Du kennst mich ja! Ich will immer alles wissen, und möglichst schnell. Also schreib mir bald wieder.

Nochmals alles Gute im neuen Jahr und viele liebe Grüße

Deine

Karin

Übungen

A. Answer the following questions in English:

1 Where does Karin usually live?
2 Where do her parents live?
3 Name two things she did when she visited them
4 Where exactly does her brother usually live and what does he do for a living?
5 Why were Karin's parents particularly pleased at Christmas this time?
6 How did Karin travel back to Vienna?
7 Where is the branch of the bank situated in which Karin works?
8 Which three birds does Karin mention in her letter and why?

B. Beantworten Sie folgende Fragen:

1 Warum hat Karin so lange nicht geschrieben?
2 Seit wann ist sie wieder zu Hause?
3 Wo hat sie ihre Weihnachtsferien verbracht?
4 Wen hat sie bei ihren Eltern wieder gesehen?
5 Wo arbeitet ihr Bruder?
6 Was ist er von Beruf?
7 Was macht Karin beruflich?
8 Wo befindet sich die Filiale der Bank, in der sie arbeitet?
9 In welcher Filiale hat sie früher gearbeitet?

C. Imagine you are Karin and answer the following questions in German:

1 In welcher Stadt arbeitest du?
2 In welchem Land arbeitet dein Bruder?
3 Wer wohnt in Kärnten?
4 Worüber haben sich deine Eltern sehr gefreut?
5 Wie bist du nach Wien zurückgefahren?
6 Wie war das Wetter in Wien, als du angekommen bist?
7 An welchem Tag bist du in Wien angekommen?
8 Wo war dein Bruder, als du nach Wien gefahren bist?
9 Was macht dir nach wie vor Spaß?

D. Complete the following letter to Manfred by filling in the blanks with the information supplied in English after the blanks. Each blank must be filled in by one German word. Refer to Karin's letter and the words and expressions in Section E to find the vocabulary you require.

Notes	
	– – (Dear Manfred),

zu – – – (your 18th birthday) gratuliere ich Dir herzlich und – – (wish you) – – (all the best) für das neue Lebensjahr. – – – – – – – (I have already sent you a parcel). Hoffentlich – – – – (it arrives in good time). – – – (Please write to me) ausführlich, – – – – – – (how you usually spend your birthday).

– – – – – – – (Christmas and the New Year are drawing closer). Heute – – – – – –, (I was in town again) und habe noch ein paar Geschenke – – – (for my brothers and sisters) – – – (and my parents) gekauft. – – – – – –. (I was however not able to accomplish everything). – – – (There were simply) – – – (too many people) – – –, (in town) und – – – – – – (I had only a little time). – – –, (In the parcel) – – – – –, (that I have sent you) ist – – – – – – (also a small Christmas present for you). – – – – (I do hope you like it).

only a little
nur ein wenig

– – – – (My parents and I) wollen – – – – – (the Christmas days at my grandparents) – – – (in the country) verbringen. – – (We shall be coming) erst – – – (on 28th December) – – – (back home). Silvester – – – – – (we want to celebrate at home).

Christmas das
Weihnachtsfest

Ich – – – – (wish you therefore once more) – – – –, (many happy returns of the day on your birthday) – – – (a merry Christmas) und natürlich einen guten Rutsch ins Neue Jahr.

Meine Eltern lassen herzlich grüßen

– (Yours)

Jennifer

E. Make sure you learn the following words and expressions:

ausführlich in detail
auf einen Haufen all at once
einfach simply
die Ente duck
erledigen finish, manage, accomplish
feiern to celebrate
das Fest feast, festival
die Filiale branch (e.g. of a bank)
frohe/fröhliche Weihnachten merry
  Christmas
ein frohes Weihnachtsfest a merry
  Christmas
die Gans goose
gewöhnlich usually
gratulieren (+ dat.) congratulate

guten Rutsch ins neue/Neue
  Jahr Happy New Year
herzliche Glückwünsche zum
  Geburtstag happy birthday, many
  happy returns of the day
hoffentlich I hope that
Kärnten Carinthia (Austrian province)
Mensch! gosh!
näherrücken draw closer
das Neujahr New Year's Day; 1st
  January
das neue/Neue Jahr the New Year
normalerweise normally
nur sehr wenig only a little
die Oper opera

das Paket parcel	**der Silvester** New Year's Eve
die Pute turkey (hen)	**Weihnachten/das**
der Puter turkey (cock)	**Weihnachtsfest** Christmas
rechtzeitig in good time	**das Weihnachtslied** Christmas carol
Ski fahren/Ski laufen to go skiing	**der Weihnachtsmann** Santa Claus,
schlimm bad	Father Christmas
Schlittschuh fahren/laufen to go ice-	**die Weihnachtskarte** Christmas card
skating	

F. Imagine you are Philip and are writing to Karin in Vienna. Read her letter and tell her how you spent Christmas. Answer all the questions in the final paragraph of her letter.

Unit 8

Hast du Lust dazu?

Leer, den 27. März

Lieber Tom!

Ich habe wieder einige deutsche Briefmarken für Dich. Vergiß bitte nicht, mir sofort zu schreiben, daß Du sie bekommen hast! Im nächsten Jahr werde ich Dir einen gebrauchten Briefmarkenkatalog schicken, damit Du Deine Briefmarken besser ordnen kannst.

gebraucht	used
ordnen	arrange
die Eßnische	dining alcove
die Diele	entrance hall
tapezieren	to wallpaper
die Tapeten	wallpaper
aussuchen	to select
fix und fertig	all ready
verschlingen	to swallow
großartig	splendid
der Vorschlag	suggestion
nichts Besonderes	nothing special

Am 9. April ziehen wir nun endlich um. Unsere neue Wohnung hat ein Wohnzimmer mit Eßnische, drei Schlafzimmer, Bad, Küche und eine Diele. Wir müssen nur noch das Wohnzimmer tapezieren. Meine Eltern haben die Tapeten schon ausgesucht und bestellt. Ansonsten ist die Wohnung fix und fertig.

Dieses Jahr können wir nicht in Urlaub fahren. Mein Vater sagt, die neue Wohnung hat viel Geld verschlungen. Wir werden also auf dem Balkon und im Garten Urlaub machen.

Meine Eltern haben mir einen großartigen Vorschlag gemacht. Ich soll Dich einladen, im Juli oder August für drei Wochen zu uns zu kommen. Hast Du Lust dazu? Oder hast Du schon andere Pläne? Unsere Stadt bietet nichts Besonderes, aber wir können schwimmen oder wandern gehen. Das Hallenbad ist nicht sehr weit von unserer neuen Wohnung, und wir haben auch ein neues Freibad. Falls Du kommen kannst, schreibe mir bitte rechtzeitig, was Du machen möchtest. Wenn Du Lust hast, ins Konzert oder Theater zu gehen, können wir mit der Bahn nach Bremen fahren. In einer Stunde ist man da. Ich hoffe sehr, daß Du kommst.

Herzliche Grüße

Dein

Rolf

Übungen

A. Answer the following questions in English:

1. What has Rolf sent to Tom and why?
2. What will Tom be getting from Rolf next year?
3. Why won't Rolf and his parents be going away on holiday this year?
4. Describe the new flat.
5. What remains to be done in the new flat?
6. What have Rolf's parents suggested to him?
7. What is there to do in Leer in the summer?
8. What does Rolf apparently do when he wants to go to the theatre?

B. Beantworten Sie folgende Fragen:

1. Was sammelt Tom?
2. Was soll er machen, wenn er die Briefmarken von Rolf bekommt?
3. Was wird ihm Rolf im nächsten Jahr schicken?
4. Warum?
5. Wann genau zieht Rolf um?
6. Wozu haben seine Eltern neue Tapeten bestellt?
7. Warum können Rolf und seine Eltern dieses Jahr nicht in Urlaub fahren?
8. Wohin fährt Rolf normalerweise, wenn er ins Konzert gehen will?
9. Wie lange dauert die Bahnfahrt von Leer nach Bremen?

C. Imagine you are Rolf and answer the following questions in German:

1. An welchem Tag haben Sie diesen Brief geschrieben?
2. Warum haben Sie Tom Briefmarken geschickt?
3. Was für Briefmarken sammelt Tom?
4. Bei wem wohnen Sie noch?
5. In welchem Monat ziehen Sie um?
6. Wer hat die Tapeten für das Wohnzimmer in der neuen Wohnung ausgesucht?
7. Wo wollen Sie dieses Jahr den Urlaub verbringen?
8. Was haben Sie Ihrem Freund Tom vorgeschlagen?
9. Wohin geht man in Leer schwimmen?

D. Translate the following letter to Rolf into German. Refer to Rolf's original letter, the notes in the margins and the words and expressions in Section E to find the vocabulary you require.

[Place and Date]

Dear Rolf,

Many thanks for your letter and the stamps. I have already bought a new album for my stamps. I am looking forward to receiving a stamp catalogue from you.

Many thanks, too, for your invitation to spend three weeks at your place in July or August. My parents have agreed to this. I shall probably fly to Bremen and then take the train to Leer. Air tickets for pupils and students cost less than the normal price.

You ask what I would like to do in Leer. I love swimming, so if the weather is good, we could go to the outdoor baths. If there is a good concert in Bremen we can go there by train. We can also go on excursions in the neighbourhood. If you have two bicycles, we could go on a cycling tour. What do you say to that?

I know you collect picture postcards. I have already collected about a hundred for you and will bring them with me when I come. If you would like anything else please write to me in good time. A postcard will do.

Once again many thanks for the invitation, all the best and regards to your parents.

> Yours
>
> Tom

> stamp album **das Briefmarkenalbum**
> invitation **die Einladung**
> have agreed to this **sind damit einverstanden**
> excursion **der Ausflug**
> the neighbourhood **die Umgebung**
> cycling tour **die Radtour**
> picture postcard **die Ansichtskarte**
> in good time **rechtzeitig**
> a postcard will do **Postkarte genügt**

E. Make sure you learn the following words and expressions:

das Album album
die Ansichtskarte picture postcard
der Ausflug excursion, outing, trip
aussuchen to select, choose
besonders especially, particularly
bestellen to order
die Diele vestibule, entrance hall (to a house or flat)
einverstanden sein (mit etwas einverstanden sein) to agree (about something)
die Eßnische dining alcove
etwas Besonderes something special, something in particular
fix und fertig all ready
das Freibad open-air swimming baths
gebrauchen to use, to make use of
gebraucht used (or second-hand)

großartig great, splendid, fabulous
das Hallenbad (indoor) swimming baths
Lust haben (hast du Lust dazu?) feel like doing something, to want to do something (would you like to do that?)
nichts Besonderes nothing special, nothing in particular
ordnen to arrange, sort
Postkarte genügt a postcard will do (or suffice)
die Radtour cycling tour
die Tapeten wallpaper
tapezieren to (wall)paper
umziehen to move house
verschlingen to swallow (up)
der Vorschlag suggestion
vorschlagen to suggest

F. Write a letter to a friend (FRY) in Germany inviting him or her to spend a few weeks with you in the summer holidays. Mention what one can do where you live and try to use as many as possible of the new words and expressions you have come across in this unit.

Unit 9

Wer ist dran?

Kassel, den 14. August

Liebe Ruth, lieber Jim!

Es tut mir furchtbar leid, daß ich nicht früher geschrieben habe, aber es ging einfach nicht. Zuerst war ich im Urlaub und dann gab es einen Todesfall in der Familie.

Meine Großmutter, die nicht mal ganz 60 Jahre alt war, starb plötzlich zwei Tage nach meiner Rückkehr. Sie erlitt einen Herzanfall am 14. Juli und starb schon im Krankenwagen auf dem Wege zum Krankenhaus. Oma hatte niemals über Herzbeschwerden geklagt, daher war ihr Tod ein großer Schock für uns alle. Die Trauerfeier fand im engsten Familienkreis statt.

Und nun zu meinem Urlaub. Ich war drei Wochen lang in Rimini in Italien. Das Wetter war herrlich, die Leute sehr freundlich und das Essen war für mich etwas Besonderes. Ich habe nie im Leben so viel gegessen: Spaghetti, Makkaroni, Cannelloni und viele andere Pastagerichte gab es jeden Tag und ich habe fast fünf Pfund zugenommen. Tagsüber war ich natürlich immer am Strand. Endlich konnte ich den ganzen Tag faulenzen und in der Sonne liegen. Als ich nach Hause zurückfuhr, war ich richtig braun. Nächstes Jahr möchte ich meinen Sommerurlaub auf Sizilien verbringen. Es soll dort sehr schön sein.

Was habt Ihr in den Ferien gemacht? Seid Ihr weggefahren oder zu Hause geblieben? Ich erwarte einen langen Brief von Euch! Ich glaube, Du mußt diesmal schreiben, Ruth! Oder bist Du dran, Jim?

Viele liebe Grüße

Euer

Reinhard

der Todesfall	death
die Rückkehr	return
der Herzanfall	heart attack
klagen über (+ acc.)	complain about
Herzbeschwerden *here:* weak heart	
die Trauerfeier	funeral
stattfinden	to take place
etwas Besonderes	something special
das Gericht	dish
zunehmen	to put on weight
tagsüber	during the day
faulenzen	to laze, be idle
oder bist du dran?	or is it your turn?

Übungen

A. Answer the following questions in English:

   1 Why did Reinhard not write earlier to Jim and Ruth?
   2 When exactly did he return home from Italy?
   3 What happened two days after he returned to Kassel?
   4 How old was Reinhard's grandmother when she died?
   5 Where did she die?
   6 Why was the family so shocked?
   7 Who attended her funeral?
   8 What did Reinhard do most of the time when he was on holiday?

B. Beantworten Sie folgende Fragen:

   1 An welchem Tag kam Reinhard vom Urlaub nach Hause zurück?
   2 Wie alt war seine Großmutter, als sie starb?
   3 Woran starb sie?
   4 Warum wußte niemand, daß sie ein schwaches Herz hatte?
   5 Wo starb sie?
   6 Wohin ging Reinhard jeden Tag, als er in Rimini war?
   7 Wozu ging er dorthin?
   8 Wie findet er die italienische Küche?

C. Imagine you are Reinhard and answer the following questions in German:

   1 Warum haben Sie diesen Brief nicht früher geschrieben?
   2 Wohin sind Sie in Urlaub gefahren?
   3 Was hat Ihnen in Italien besonders gut gefallen?
   4 Warum haben Sie so viel zugenommen?
   5 Wie kommt es, daß Sie schon nach drei Wochen so braun geworden sind?
   6 Was sind Ihre Pläne für die nächsten Sommerferien?
   7 Wo liegt Sizilien?
   8 Was für einen Brief möchten Sie nun von Ruth oder Jim bekommen?

D. Complete the following letter to Reinhard by filling in the blanks with the information provided in English after the blanks. Each blank must be filled in by one German word. Refer to Reinhard's original letter and the words and expressions in Section E to find the vocabulary you require.

– – (Dear Reinhard)!

Du hast – (for a long time) nicht – – (from us) – (heard), aber wir sind erst – – – (four days ago) aus – – (our holiday) zurückgekommen. – – –, (Your letter came) als – – – (we were away).

– – (This year) – – (we were) – – (in the south of France) und zwar in Cap d'Ail an der französischen Riviera. – – (We had) – – – – (a very nice room) – – – (in a small) Pension – – – – (not far from the beach). – – – –, (The food was excellent) aber – – – (the portions were) – – – (unfortunately too small). Ich glaube, ich habe – – – (lost four pounds). Ruth hat natürlich nicht abgenommen, denn – – – – (she eats little as it is). Die Hauptsache ist, – – – – – (that we had good weather).

– – – (And now something) – – (completely different). – – – (We now have) – – (a car). – – – – (Shortly before the holidays) habe ich meinen Führerschein gemacht. – – – (Today Ruth has) – – – (her last but one driving lesson) und macht – – (next week) – – (the driving test). – – – (I naturally drive) – – (very carefully) – – – –, (particularly in the town centre) wo – – – – (there is a lot of traffic). Deshalb – – – (the car has) – – – – – (still no dent or scratch. Fürs Autofahren jedoch – – (I must) stets – – (spectacles) aufsetzen. – –, (Ruth thinks) – – – (they suit me) ausgezeichnet.

So, das wär's für heute.

– – (All the best) – – – (from both of us).

Dein

Jim

E. Make sure you learn the following words and expressions:

abnehmen to lose weight
ausgezeichnet/prima excellent
besonders especially, particularly
die Beule dent (*but, on people*: boil, lump, swelling)
die Brille (pair of) spectacles
das wär's für heute that will be/is all for today (I think)
etwas Besonderes something special
die Fahrprüfung driving test
die Fahrstunde driving lesson
der Führerschein driving licence

den Führerschein machen to learn to drive, to take the driving test
der Familienkreis family circle
im engsten Familienkreis strictly within the family
faulenzen to be lazy, to laze, be idle
das Gericht dish
die Hauptsache the main thing
das Herz heart
der Herzanfall heart attack
die Herzbeschwerden (pl.) heart complaints

jedoch however	**stets** always, constantly, continually
leider unfortunately	**der Strand** beach
die Pension guesthouse	**tagsüber** during the day
die Riviera the Riviera	**der Todesfall** death
die Rückkehr return	**die Trauerfeier** funeral
die Schramme scratch	**der Verkehr** traffic
Sizilien Sicily	**(der vorletzte ...)** (second last, last but one)
sowieso in any case	
stattfinden to take place	**vorsichtig** carefully
stehen (+ dat.) (das steht mir nicht) to suit, attire (that does not suit me)	**wer ist dran?** whose turn is it?
	zunehmen to put on weight
sterben to die	**die Zwillinge** twins

F. Write a letter to your friends Helga and Karl who are twins (plural FRY) living in Nuremberg, saying how you spent your last summer holidays. Use Reinhard's letter to Ruth and Jim as a guide.

Unit 10

Hochzeit

Wir heiraten am 3. September 1983 in Trier

Jutta Herdzin   Karl Schmidt

Karl-Marx-Straße 15
5500 Trier

Moselstraße 27
5500 Trier

Kirchliche Trauung um 16.30 Uhr im Dom
Polterabend: 1. September 1983 ab 19.30 Uhr
in der Gaststätte „Zur Krone",
Bruchhausenstraße 14.

Übungen

A. Answer the following questions in English:

1 When did Jutta Herdzin and Karl Schmidt get married?
2 Where exactly did they get married?
3 Where did the 'Polterabend' take place?
4 At what time did the Polterabend commence?
5 At what time did the marriage ceremony commence?
6 Why are three streets mentioned in the wedding card?

B. Beantworten Sie folgende Fragen:

1 Wann haben Jutta Herdzin und Karl Schmidt geheiratet?
2 Wo hatte Jutta gewohnt, bevor sie heiratete?
3 In welcher Straße befand sich Karls Wohnung?
4 Wo genau fand die kirchliche Trauung statt?
5 Um wieviel Uhr?
6 Ab wieviel Uhr durften die Gäste zum Polterabend kommen?
7 In welcher Straße befindet sich die Gaststätte, in der der Polterabend stattgefunden hat?

C. Translate the following letter into German. Refer to Jutta's wedding card, the notes in the margin and the words and expressions in Section D to find the vocabulary you require. Remember you are writing to two friends who are married.

Trier, 15th June

Dear Erika and Hermann,

My brother is getting married to Jutta on 3rd September. At first he wanted only a registry office marriage ceremony, but Jutta wanted to get married in the cathedral, so they will have a church wedding after all. This will take place on 3rd September at 4.30 pm in the cathedral in Trier. The Polterabend is taking place on 1st September in the Crown restaurant. I think we had dinner there once when you visited us last year at Easter. The restaurant is in the Bruchhausenstraße.

to get married to	**heiraten**
registry office marriage	**die**
	standesamtliche Trauung
church wedding	**die**
	kirchliche Trauung
Polterabend	*see* Section D
to take place	**stattfinden**
restaurant	*use:* **die Gaststätte**
is located in	**befindet sich**
	in
wedding	**die Hochzeit**
now	*use:* **schon jetzt**
to take time off	
work	**freinehmen**
honeymoon	**die**
	Flitterwochen (pl.)
Turkey	**die Türkei**
prize	**der Preis**
photographic competition	
	der Fotowettbewerb
lucky person/devil	**der**
	Glückspilz

All of us would be very pleased if you could come to the wedding. If possible try to be here for the Polterabend. Of course you can stay with us. There is plenty of room in the house. I am writing to you now so that you can take a few days off in good time.

By the way, Karl and Jutta want to spend their honeymoon in Turkey. Karl has just won the first prize in a photographic competition — DM2000. He really is a lucky devil. So they can afford to go to Turkey. Do let me know soon whether you are coming or not.

All the best

Yours

Heino

D. Make sure you learn the following words and expressions:

der Dom cathedral
eben just
die Ermäßigung reduction in price
die Flitterwochen (pl.) honeymoon
das Foto photograph
der Fotowettbewerb photographic competition
freinehmen to take time off
die Gaststätte restaurant
der Glückspilz lucky person/devil
heiraten to marry, get married
die Hochzeit (*or* **Vermählung)** wedding
die kirchliche Trauung church marriage ceremony

sich leisten to be able to afford
poltern to rumble, make a racket
der Polterabend party which is held on the eve or two days before the wedding at which crockery is smashed to frighten away evil spirits.
der Preis prize
das Standesamt registry office
die standesamtliche Trauung registry office marriage ceremony
die Trauung marriage ceremony
die Türkei Turkey
der Wettbewerb competition

Unit 11

Es ist endlich soweit!

Preston, den 16. Juni

Liebe Birgit!

So, es ist endlich soweit! Heute nachmittag habe ich meine Fahrkarten vom Reisebüro abgeholt. Stell Dir mal vor, sie waren gar nicht so teuer. Für die Rückfahrkarte nach Köln habe ich ungefähr DM200,– bezahlt. Ich habe natürlich verbilligte Karten gekriegt, da ich einen Studentenausweis habe.

Und nun zu meiner Reise. Ich fahre am Samstagmorgen, dem 12. Juli hier los. Mein Vater bringt mich zum Bahnhof, denn der Zug nach London fährt um 04.17 Uhr ab. Um 09.31 Uhr bin ich in London und muß dann mit der U-Bahn nach Victoria weiterfahren. Von dort aus muß ich mit dem Zug nach Dover. Um 13.20 Uhr (englische Zeit) nehme ich den Jetfoil d.h. das Tragflügelboot nach Oostende. Die Überfahrt dauert ca. zwei Stunden. Um 16 Uhr (mitteleuropäische Zeit) bin ich schon in Oostende und fahre dann um 16.43 Uhr mit dem Zug in Richtung Köln. Ich komme dort um 20.17 Uhr an und nehme an, Du holst mich vom Bahnhof ab. Wenn es nicht geht, nehme ich ein Taxi.

Ich will nur einen kleinen Koffer mitbringen, denn ich habe keine Lust, viel Gepäck mitzuschleppen. Mein Vater sagt immer: Gepäck aufgeben ist besser als Gepäck mitschleppen. Ich sage: je weniger, desto besser.

Ich werde auch die Dias von Deinem Besuch bei uns im vorigen Jahr mitbringen. Übrigens habe ich jetzt einen nagelneuen Fotoapparat, den ich von meinen Eltern zum Geburtstag bekommen habe, und bringe ihn selbstverständlich mit.

Viele Grüße and alles Gute

Dein

Jack

es ist soweit	everything is settled
stell dir mal vor	just imagine
verbilligt	at reduced rates
das Tragflügelboot	jetfoil
die Überfahrt	the crossing
ca. (circa)	about
annehmen	to assume
mitschleppen	to carry, drag along
Gepäck aufgeben	to send luggage in advance
das Dia	slide

Übungen

A. Answer the following questions in English:

1 What did Jack do on the afternoon of 16th June?
2 Why didn't he have to pay the full price for the tickets he bought?
3 What kind of ticket did he buy and how much did it cost?
4 When precisely is he leaving for Germany?
5 What will he have to do when his train arrives in London?
6 What will his route be from Victoria onwards?
7 What is his final destination and what time will he arrive there?
8 Why does he mention the taxi in his letter?

B. Beantworten Sie folgende Fragen:

1 Wann hat Jack die Fahrkarten gekauft?
2 Wo hat er sie bekommen?
3 Warum konnte er verbilligte Fahrkarten bekommen?
4 Wie will er zum Bahnhof in Preston fahren?
5 Was muß er in London tun, wenn er dort ankommt?
6 Wie will er nach Victoria fahren?
7 Wie lange war Jack von Preston nach Köln unterwegs?
8 Wo in Deutschland wohnt seine Freundin?
9 Was will er machen, falls Birgit ihn nicht abholen kann?

C. Imagine you are Jack and answer the following questions in German:

1 Was hast du heute nachmittag gemacht?
2 Was hast du für die Fahrkarten ausgegeben?
3 Warum hast du eine Ermäßigung gekriegt?
4 Wie fährst du von Oostende nach Köln?
5 Wie lange mußt du in Oostende warten, bevor dein Zug abfährt?
6 Was für Gepäck willst du mitnehmen?
7 Wozu willst du deinen Fotoapparat mitnehmen?
8 Wann hast du diesen Fotoapparat bekommen?

D. Translate the following letter into German. Refer to Jack's original letter, the notes in the margins and the words and expressions in Section E to find the vocabulary you require.

Shrewsbury, 18th June

Dear Ingrid,

This morning I picked up my tickets from the travel agency. At last I know when I am flying. I am setting off from here on 22nd July. My mother is taking me to the railway station as the train leaves very early — at 06.50. The train arrives in London at 09.55. I must then travel to Heathrow airport on the Underground. My plane does not leave until 13.10 so I have plenty of time. I am flying Lufthansa and we shall be making a stopover in Cologne. The plane (Flight No. LH 238) lands in Zurich at 17.25. I hope you will pick me up at the airport.

I shall be bringing only a small suitcase as I have no desire to carry a lot of baggage. The main thing is that I do not forget my swimming costume and my camera! I hope the weather in Switzerland is good in July and August.

I have already booked my return flight. I shall be flying back to London on 10th August. My plane leaves at 10 o'clock in the morning. So now you know my plans. Please write to me in good time in case you require anything from here.

With love

Patricia

at last	**endlich**
to set off	**losfahren**
I am flying …	**ich fliege mit der …**
stopover	**die Zwischenlandung**
to land	**landen**
Flight No. (Number)	**(die) Flug-Nr. (Nummer)**
the main thing	**die Hauptsache**
to book	**buchen**
in case	**falls**

E. Make sure you learn the following words and expressions:

abholen to pick up
annehmen to assume
der Ausweis identity card
der Badeanzug swimming costume
die Badehose swimming trunks
buchen to book
circa (ca.) about, approximately
das Dia (pl: Dias) slide, colour transparency
endlich at last
es ist endlich soweit everything is settled at last
der Flug flight
der Flughafen airport
der Fotoapparat camera
das Gepäck baggage, luggage
Gepäck aufgeben to send luggage in advance
die Hauptsache the main (or most important) thing
je weniger, desto besser the less the better

Köln Cologne
kriegen to get, obtain, receive
landen to land
die Landung landing
losfahren set off
die Lufthansa German national airline
mitschleppen to drag along
mitteleuropäische Zeit (abbrev. MEZ) Central European Time (one hour ahead of British time)
nagelneu brand new
rechtzeitig in good time
das Reisebüro travel agency
der Rückflug return flight
die Schweiz Switzerland
selbstverständlich of course, naturally
der Studentenausweis student identity card
das Tragflügelboot jetfoil
die Überfahrt crossing
die U-Bahn (Untergrundbahn) underground, tube

übrigens by the way, incidentally	**verbilligt** at reduced rates or price
ungefähr about, roughly, approximately	**Zürich** Zurich
	die Zwischenlandung stopover

F. Imagine you are going to visit a friend in Heidelberg. Ask your local travel agent to give you the relevant air/rail/coach timetables to plan your trip from where you live to your destination in Germany. Find out how much it would cost and write to your friend saying how you will be travelling. Read Jack's letter to Birgit again before drafting your letter and use as many of the words and expressions in this unit as you can.

Unit 12

Es läßt sich nicht ändern!

Aberdeen, den 21. Juni

Liebe Ulla,

es tut mir leid, daß ich dieses Jahr nun doch nicht zu Dir kommen kann. Meine Mutter liegt seit einer Woche im Krankenhaus, und da mein Vater allein zu Hause ist, muß ich für ihn sorgen.

Meine Mutter muß mindestens noch sechs Wochen im Krankenhaus bleiben. Das ist die Folge eines Verkehrsunfalls. Am vorigen Samstag war sie in der Stadt, um einzukaufen. Da passierte es. Als sie aus dem Supermarkt kam und über die Straße ging, fuhr ein Autofahrer sie an. Meine Mutter ist nicht sicher, was dann geschah. Auf einmal lag sie mitten auf der Straße. Der Unfallwagen brachte sie zum Krankenhaus. Dort stellten die Ärzte fest, daß ihr rechtes Bein gebrochen war. Ich sage Dir, niemand ist heutzutage im Straßenverkehr sicher. Meine Mutter ist sowieso immer ein Pechvogel. Vor zwei Jahren fiel sie die Treppe hinunter und brach sich dabei den linken Arm. Damals mußte sie zwei Monate im Krankenhaus verbringen, denn sie hatte auch schwere Kopfverletzungen erlitten.

Ich bin natürlich sehr enttäuscht, daß ich nicht kommen kann, aber es läßt sich nicht ändern. Frag doch Deine Eltern, ob ich nächstes Jahr kommen darf! Wenn es nicht geht, werde ich in die Schweiz fahren, um einen früheren Schulfreund zu besuchen. Wir haben uns seit viereinhalb Jahren nicht gesehen.

Viele Grüße an Dich und Deine Eltern!

Deine

Carol

doch *here:* after all
sorgen für too look after/to take care of
mindestens at least
die Folge result
anfahren to run into/to collide with
feststellen to find out
heutzutage nowadays
der Pechvogel unlucky person
es läßt sich nicht ändern it can't be helped
die Schweiz Switzerland

Übungen

A. Answer the following questions in English:

1 Why won't Carol be going to Germany as planned?
2 How did her mother break her leg?
3 How long will she have been in hospital if she is discharged as planned?
4 Why does Carol call her mother an unlucky person?
5 Why is Carol disappointed?
6 What does she suggest to Ulla?
7 What will Carol do if Ulla says this is not possible?

B. Beantworten Sie folgende Fragen:

1 Warum kann Carol dieses Jahr nicht zu Ulla fahren?
2 Warum liegt ihre Mutter im Krankenhaus?
3 Wo passierte der Unfall?
4 Wo hatte Carols Mutter gerade eingekauft?
5 Wo befand sie sich, als der Autofahrer sie anfuhr?
6 Wo stellten die Ärzte fest, daß ihr rechtes Bein gebrochen war?
7 In welchem Land will Carol nächstes Jahr ihren Urlaub verbringen, wenn sie auch dann nicht zu Ulla fahren kann?

C. Imagine you are Carol and answer the following questions in German:

1 Für wen mußt du sorgen, da deine Mutter im Krankenhaus liegt?
2 Wohin ging deine Mutter, um einzukaufen, gerade bevor der Unfall passierte?
3 Wie kam sie zum Krankenhaus?
4 Wann darf sie wahrscheinlich nach Hause gehen?
5 Wann durfte sie das Krankenhaus verlassen, als sie ihren Arm gebrochen hatte?
6 Wohin möchtest du nächstes Jahr fahren?
7 Wer wohnt in der Schweiz?
8 Wann hast du ihn zuletzt gesehen?

D. Complete the following letter to Carol by filling in the blanks with the information supplied after the blanks. Each blank must be filled in by one word. Refer to Carol's original letter to Ulla and the words and expressions in Section E to find the vocabulary you require.

Notes	
	– – (Dear Carol)!

– – – – – (We are very sorry) – –, (to hear) – – – – – – (that your mother is lying in hospital). – – (She is) tatsächlich – –, (an unlucky person) aber was für ein Glück, – – – – – – (that she is not injured seriously). Hoffentlich – – – – (her leg is healing well). – – – – (My parents and I) – – (wish her) gute Besserung, und hoffen, – – – – – – (that she is soon in good health again).

– – –, (Of course we understand) – – – – – – (that you can't come now). – – – – – –, (You are probably finding it very difficult) ohne Deine Mutter zurechtzukommen. – – – – – – – – – (I have spoken to my parents about your suggestion). – – – – – –, (I'm afraid it won't be possible in the summer) – – – – – (for my parents and I) – – – – – – – (want to go to Spain for four weeks). – – –, (My mother says) – – – – – (you could come at Easter)! – – – – (What do you say to that)? – – – – –, (We would be very pleased) – – – – (to see you here again). – – – (I do hope it works out).

possible es geht

here bei uns
works out es klappt

– – – – – – – (By the way we now have an Alsatian again). – – – – – (He is six months old) – – – – – (and very well-behaved and clever). – – – (He is called Fanto).

– – – – – – –, (So once again all the best for your mother) und herzliche Grüße – – – – – (to her and to your father).

– – – (Write again soon)

– (Yours)

Ulla

E. Make sure you learn the following words and expressions:

anfahren to run into, to collide with	**hoffentlich klappt es** I do hope it works out
brav well-behaved	
erleiden to suffer	**die Kopfverletzung** head injury
enttäuscht sein to be disappointed	**leider** unfortunately
es läßt sich nicht ändern it can't be helped	**mindestens** at least
	der Pechvogel unlucky person
feststellen to ascertain, to find out	**der Schäferhund** Alsatian ('German Shepherd' dog)
die Folge result	
es geht nicht it is not possible	**die Schweiz** Switzerland
gute Besserung get well soon (**ich wünsche dir gute Besserung**) (I wish you a speedy recovery)	**sorgen für** to take care of, to look after
	Spanien Spain
	übrigens by the way; incidentally
heilen to heal	**der Unfallwagen** ambulance
heutzutage nowadays	**der Verkehrsunfall** traffic accident
	der Vorschlag suggestion

vorschlagen to suggest	**wohlauf sein** to be in good health
Was für ein Glück! What luck!/How fortunate!	**zurechtkommen** to manage, to be able to manage

F. Three weeks before you are supposed to travel to Germany with your brother, he is involved in a road accident while riding his bicycle. You have to cancel your trip and are now writing to your penfriend Günter in Koblenz, saying that you will not be able to visit him this year as planned. Give him your reasons and describe the accident in which your brother was involved in detail. Read Carol's letter to Ulla again before writing your letter and remember to use as many of the new words and expressions in this unit as you can.

Unit 13

Oma ist gestorben!

Meine liebe Frau, unsere gute Mutter, Schwiegermutter,
Großmutter, Urgroßmutter, Schwägerin und Tante

Frieda Wadephul
geb. Dill

wurde heute von Gott unserem Herrn im Alter von 88 Jahren heimgerufen.

Walter Wadephul
Vera Bräuniger, geb. Wadephul
Prof. Dr. Harald Bräuniger
DDR 25 Rostock, Schliemannstraße 27
Karin Wadephul, geb. Schäfer
Werner Wadephul
2249 Westerwohld
Heidi Spiekermann, geb. Eichmann
Lutz Spiekermann
Plön/Ostholstein
Acht Enkel und acht Urenkel

2000 Hamburg 76, 20. November 1981
Finkenau 19
Am Husarendenkmal 49

Die Trauerfeier findet am Montag, dem 30. November 1981, um 14 Uhr in der Kapelle des Blankeneser Friedhofes in Sülldorf, Sülldorfer Kirchenweg (Bus 187) statt.

Übungen

A. Answer the following questions in English:

1 How old was Mrs Frieda Wadephul when she died?
2 What was her maiden name?
3 How many grandchildren and great-grandchildren did she leave behind?
4 When did she die?
5 When did the funeral take place?
6 Where did it take place?
7 How do you get to the cemetery where she is buried if you don't have a car?
8 What is the full name of Mrs Wadephul's husband?
9 Where does Professor Harald Bräuniger live?

B. Beantworten Sie folgende Fragen:

1. Wie hieß die Dame, die verstorben ist?
2. In welcher Stadt starb sie?
3. Wann ist sie gestorben?
4. Wie alt wurde sie?
5. Wie heißt ihr Ehemann?
6. Wieviele Enkel und wieviele Urenkel hatte sie?
7. Wo wohnt Prof. Dr. Harald Bräuniger?
8. Wo fand die Trauerfeier statt?
9. Wann und um wieviel Uhr fand sie statt?
10. Mit welcher Buslinie erreicht man den Friedhof?

C. Imagine you are Mrs Frieda Wadephul's granddaughter Karin. Refer to the card announcing her death, the notes in the margin and the words and expressions in Section E to find the vocabulary you require to translate the following letter to the Graham family into German. Use the formal 'Sie' form in your letter.

Hamburg, 27th November

Dear Familie Graham,

I have some very sad news for you. My grandmother Frieda died a week ago. She was 88 years old. For some time she had been quite ill. As you know she and my grandfather had been living in an old people's home for two years. However, we were able to visit them frequently. My grandfather is still living at the home, but he is alone now and this is definitely not easy for him. He is over 89 years old but still quite active for his age. Until about two years ago he was still riding through the neighbourhood on his bicycle. I found this fabulous and admire him a lot.

The death of my grandmother is a great loss for all of us, but of course, especially for him. They were happily married for fifty-two years. Two years ago they celebrated their golden wedding anniversary in grand style. It was wonderful!

I hope you are all well! I shall write to you again after the funeral on 30th November.

Yours sincerely,

Karin

some very sad news	**eine ganz traurige Nachricht**
for some time	**seit einiger Zeit**
old people's home	**das Altenheim**
frequently	**häufig**
quite active	**ganz rüstig**
age	**das Alter**
through the neighbourhood	**durch die Gegend**
to admire	**bewundern**
death	**der Tod**
loss	**der Verlust**
married	**verheiratet**
to celebrate	**feiern**
golden wedding anniversary	**die goldene Hochzeit**
in grand style	**im großen Stil**

D. Make sure you learn the following words and expressions:

das Altenheim/Altersheim home for old people	**im Alter von** at the age of
das Alter age	**die Beerdigung** burial, funeral
	bewundern to admire

die DDR (Deutsche Demokratische Republik)   German Democratic Republic (East Germany)
der Ehemann   husband
der Enkel   grandson/grandchild
feiern   celebrate
der Friedhof   cemetery
geb. (= geboren)   née
heimgerufen   *here:* called home by God
die Hochzeit   wedding
die goldene Hochzeit   golden wedding anniversary

die Kapelle   chapel
(die) Oma   grandma, granny
(der) Opa   grandpa, grandad
rüstig   active
der Schwager   brother-in-law
die Schwägerin   sister-in-law
die Schwiegermutter   mother-in-law
stattfinden   to take place
der Stil   style
die Trauerfeier   funeral service
die Urgroßmutter   great-grandmother
der Urenkel   great-grandson/grandchild
der Verlust   loss

Keine Übernachtung ohne Bettwäsche!

Jane Graham

3 Coniston Crescent
Workington
Cumbria CA14 3NL
England

den 15. Mai 1983

Jugendherberge
Meerwiesertalweg 31

D-6600 Saarbrücken

Sehr geehrter Herr!

Hiermit möchte ich sechs Betten für die Zeit vom 19. Juli bis zum 22. Juli 1983, d.h. für drei Übernachtungen reservieren. Unsere Gruppe besteht aus drei Jungen und drei Mädchen und wir sind alle siebzehn Jahre alt. Wir hoffen, am 19. Juli gegen 17.30 Uhr anzukommen, und beabsichtigen, am 22. Juli gleich nach dem Frühstück abzureisen. Wir sind alle im Besitz eines Jugendherbergsausweises.

Wir möchten von Ihnen Bettwäsche leihen, da wir keine Leinen- oder Nesselschlafsäcke besitzen. Hoffentlich geht das!

Teilen Sie mir bitte mit, welche Mahlzeiten man bei Ihnen erhalten kann. Wir möchten in der Jugendherberge frühstücken und zu Abend essen.

Für eine baldige Antwort wäre ich Ihnen dankbar. Ein internationaler Postantwortschein liegt bei.

Mit freundlichen Grüßen

Jane Graham

bestehen aus	consist of
im Besitz sein	hold, be in possession of
der Ausweis	membership card or identity card
leihen	hire/borrow
mitteilen	inform, communicate (to)
der Leinenschlafsack	linen sheet sleeping bag
der Nesselschlafsack	cotton fabric sleeping bag
besitzen	possess

Übungen

A. Answer the following questions in English:

1 Why has Jane Graham written to the youth hostel in Saarbrücken?
2 With whom is she travelling to Germany?
3 When do they hope to arrive at the youth hostel?
4 How long do they intend staying in Saarbrücken?
5 What has Jane sent with her letter and why?
6 What kind of sleeping bags are visitors permitted to use in a German youth hostel?
7 What information has Jane asked the warden of the youth hostel to send her?
8 Why does she want this information?

B. Beantworten Sie folgende Fragen:

1 Warum hat Jane Graham an die Jugendherberge in Saarbrücken geschrieben?
2 Wo befindet sich die Jugendherberge in Saarbrücken?
3 Wieviele Personen wollen Jane begleiten, wenn sie im Sommer nach Deutschland fährt?
4 Wann will die Gruppe in der Jugendherberge ankommen?
5 Warum müssen die Mädchen Bettwäsche entleihen?
6 Was soll der Herbergsvater Jane mitteilen?
7 Was legt Jane ihrem Brief bei?
8 Warum hat sie das gemacht?

C. Imagine you are Jane and answer the following questions:

1 In welcher Jugendherberge willst du am 20. Juli übernachten?
2 Mit wem willst du nach Saarbrücken fahren?
3 Um wieviel Uhr wollt ihr in der Jugendherberge ankommen?
4 Wann genau wollt ihr abreisen?
5 Was mußt du unbedingt haben, wenn du in einer Jugendherberge übernachten willst?
6 Was für Schlafsäcke darf man in einer deutschen Jugendherberge benutzen?
7 Was darf man in einer Jugendherberge nicht tun, wenn man keine Bettwäsche hat?

D. Refer to Jane Graham's letter to the youth hostel in Saarbrücken, the notes in the margins and the words and expressions in Section E to find the vocabulary you require to translate the following letter to the youth hostel in Göttingen. (Address: Habichtsweg 2, 3400 Göttingen). Begin your first paragraph with *Hiermit*.

[Address]
[Date]

Dear Sir,

I would like to reserve two beds from 2nd August to 4th August, 1985 i.e. for two nights, for my sister and myself. My sister is sixteen years old and I am eighteen. We both possess Youth Hostel membership cards.

We are going on a cycling tour in the Federal Republic in August and hope to arrive at the Youth Hostel in Göttingen around 6 pm on 2nd August. We want to leave on 4th August right after breakfast.

We would like to hire bed linen from you as we shall be travelling without sleeping bags. We would like to have breakfast at the youth hostel. I hope this is possible.

I am enclosing an international advance booking voucher as a deposit and hope to hear from you soon.

Yours faithfully,

Hilary Benison

E. Make sure you learn the following words and expressions:

der Anmeldegutschein advance booking voucher
beabsichtigen to intend (doing)
beide both
begleiten to accompany
beilegen to enclose
benutzen to use
besitzen to own or possess, to hold
im Besitz sein to be in possession of, to hold; to be the holder of
bestehen aus (+ dat.) consist of
die Bettwäsche bed linen
entleihen (von) to borrow (from)
erhalten to get or receive
der Gutschein (über) voucher (for)
das heißt (d.h.) that is (i.e.)
der Herbergsvater youth hostel warden
die Herbergsmutter female warden
internationaler Anmeldegutschein international advance booking voucher issued by the International Youth Hostel Federation
internationaler Postantwortschein international postal reply coupon
die Jugendherberge youth hostel
der Jugendherbergsausweis Youth Hostels Association membership card
der Jugendherbergsverband Youth Hostels Association
leihen (von) to hire or borrow (from)
der Leinen linen
der Leinenschlafsack linen sheet sleeping bag
mitteilen to inform/communicate (to)
der Nessel cotton cloth
der Nesselschlafsack cotton sleeping bag
die Radtour cycling trip
verreisen to go on a journey, travel
vorhaben to plan; to intend (doing)

F. Write a letter to the youth hostel in Leer (Address: Süderkreuzstraße 7, 2950 Leer), one of the most modern youth hostels in Europe, where it is advisable to book in advance if you are going to stay there in the summer. Say you want to reserve four beds for two nights and give the approximate time of arrival and departure. Your group consists of two boys and two girls and you are all in possession of youth hostel membership cards but only two of you will be carrying sleeping bags. Say you are enclosing an international advance booking voucher and an international postal reply coupon. You will find all the words and expressions you require in this unit.

Unit 15

Teilen Sie mir Ihre Bedingungen mit!

Martin Gray

17 Belmont Terrace
Douglas
Isle of Man

den 14. August 83

Hotel Adler
Rathausplatz

A-6020 Innsbruck

Sehr geehrte Herren!

Unser Deutschlehrer Herr Parnell hat uns Ihr Hotel empfohlen. Mein Bruder und ich möchten gern unseren Skiurlaub bei Ihnen verbringen. Mein Bruder ist achtzehn Jahre alt und ich bin sechzehn. Wir brauchen ein Doppelzimmer mit Dusche für die Zeit vom 3.12. (Anreisetag) bis zum 17.12.1983 (Abreisetag).

Ich würde mich freuen, wenn Sie mir umgehend mitteilen könnten, ob Sie für uns ein Doppelzimmer reservieren können, und ob Sie eine Anzahlung verlangen.

Bitte teilen Sie mir auch folgendes mit: Ihre Bedingungen für Voll- und Halbpension sowie für Übernachtung mit Frühstück einschließlich Bedienung.

Falls Sie kein Zimmer für uns haben, wäre ich Ihnen sehr dankbar, wenn Sie mir ein anderes Hotel empfehlen könnten.

Mit freundlichen Grüßen

Martin Gray

empfehlen to recommend
verbringen to spend (time etc.)
die Dusche shower
der Anreisetag day of arrival
der Abreisetag day of departure
umgehend at your earliest convenience
mitteilen inform, communicate (to)
die Anzahlung deposit
folgendes the following, what follows
die Bedingungen terms
die Vollpension full board
die Halbpension half board
die Übernachtung a night's stay
die Bedienung service
einschließlich including
ich wäre Ihnen dankbar I would be grateful to you

Übungen

A. Answer the following questions in English:

1 How did Martin hear of this hotel?
2 Where is he going in December and why?
3 With whom is he going?
4 What sort of accommodation are they looking for?
5 How many nights will they be spending in Innsbruck?
6 Why does Martin mention the deposit in his letter to the hotel?
7 What information does Martin require from the hotel about meals?
8 What has he requested the management of the hotel to do in the event that no room is available in December?

B. Beantworten Sie folgende Fragen:

1 Wer hat Martin das Hotel empfohlen?
2 In welcher Stadt ist das Hotel?
3 Mit wem will Martin in Urlaub fahren?
4 Wie alt sind die Brüder?
5 Was für ein Zimmer hat Martin bestellt?
6 Was wollen die Brüder in Innsbruck machen?
7 Wie lange wollen sie dort bleiben?
8 Was muß Martin machen, falls der Hoteldirektor eine Anzahlung verlangt?
9 Welche Bedingungen soll der Hoteldirektor ihm mitteilen?
10 Was soll der Direktor machen, wenn er kein Zimmer für Martin und seinen Bruder hat?

C. Imagine you are Martin and answer the following questions:

1 Von wem hast du die Adresse dieses Hotels bekommen?
2 Wohin willst du im Dezember fahren?
3 Mit wem?
4 Wann wollt ihr in Innsbruck ankommen?
5 Was für ein Zimmer braucht ihr?
6 Wo liegt das Hotel Adler in Innsbruck?
7 Wann werdet ihr nach Hause zurückfahren?
8 Was machst du, wenn das Hotel kein Zimmer für euch hat?

D. Complete the following letter to the Bahnhofshotel, Bahnhofsplatz 8, in Bremen (Postleitzahl 2800), by filling in the blanks with the information supplied in English after the blanks. Each blank must be filled in by one word. Refer to the letter to the Adler Hotel and the words and expressions in Section E to find the vocabulary you require.

[Your name]   [Your address]
                                                 [Date]

[Name and Address
of Hotel]

Notes

– – – (Dear Sirs!)

Hiermit – – (I would like) – – (two single rooms) für die Zeit – –
– (from 2nd August) – – – – – (up to 16th August, 1983) – – – – –
(for my mother and myself) reservieren. Wir brauchen – – –
(two quiet rooms) – – – (around forty Marks) pro Zimmer und
Übernachtung. – – (We are flying) – – – (on 2nd August) – – (to
Bremen) und die Maschine – – – – – (lands there at 5.55 pm). –
– – (We would therefore) – – (our evening meal) – – – (in your
hotel) einnehmen. – – – (On 16th August) – – (we want to) – – –
– – (depart right after breakfast).

– – – – –, (I would be very grateful to you) wenn – – – – – – – –,
(you would inform me as soon as possible) ob Sie – – – – – –
(can reserve two single rooms for us). Bitte geben Sie mir
Bescheid, ob – – – – (you require a deposit). Da wir – (during
the day) – – –, (want to go on excursions) möchten wir – – – –
(only breakfast and evening meal) – – – (in your hotel) – (have).
Teilen Sie mir bitte – – (your terms) – – (for half-board)
einschließlich Bedienung und Mehrwertsteuer mit.

– – – – –, (I would be very pleased) wenn Sie mir – – (a town
map) – – – – – (and the theatre programme for August) – –
(could send).

Yours faithfully,

[Name and signature]

Notes

von dem   **vom**
zu dem   **zum**
an dem   **am**

around   **um**

E. Make sure you know the following words and expressions
before attempting the next exercise:

der Abreisetag day of departure
also therefore
der Anreisetag day of arrival
das Bad bath, bathroom
die Bedienung service
die Bedingungen terms or conditions
**Bescheid geben (geben Sie mir
   Bescheid)** let (a person) know,
   inform (let me know)
bestellen book, reserve
das Doppelzimmer double room
die Dusche shower
einnehmen to have (a meal), eat
   (food)
einschließlich including, inclusive of

das Einzelzimmer single room
empfehlen to recommend
folgendes the following, what follows
die Halbpension half board
hiermit herewith, hereby
die Hotelliste or **das
   Hotelverzeichnis** list of hotels
der Hotelführer hotel guide (booklet)
ich wäre Ihnen dankbar I would be
   grateful to you
ich würde mich freuen I would be
   pleased
die Insel Man Isle of Man
die Mehrwertsteuer (MWSt.) value
   added tax (VAT)

(jm. etwas) mitteilen (teilen Sie mir Ihre Bedingungen mit) inform (a person of something) (let me know your terms and conditions)	**tagsüber** during the day
	die Übernachtung (pro Übernachtung) a night's stay (per night)
reservieren reserve	**um (30,– DM)** around (thirty Marks)
ruhig quiet	**verbringen** spend (time, *not* money)
so bald wie möglich as soon as possible	**die Vollpension** full board
der Stadtplan town map	**das Verkehrsamt** tourist information office

F. Write a letter to the Tourist Information Office in Berlin (das Verkehrsamt Berlin, Europa-Center, 1000 Berlin 30, West Berlin), saying you would like to book a double room for your parents and a single room for yourself in a small and quiet hotel, for two weeks in the summer. Give the dates, saying when you will be arriving and departing.

Begin the first paragraph with **hiermit** and use the following words and expressions in your letter:

reservieren — für die Zeit — mit Bad — mit Dusche — Halbpension — Anreisetag *or* **ankommen — Abreiseisetag** *or* **abreisen — einschließlich Bedienung und Mehrwertsteuer — dankbar — schicken — Konzertprogramm — Hotelführer — geben Sie mir Bescheid — Anzahlung**

Unit 16

Schadenersatz

MAX SCHAEFER
Haffkruger Weg 35
2000 Hamburg 73

den 2.9.1983

Atlas-Reisen
Wandsbeker Marktstraße 96

2000 Hamburg 70

Betreff: Kreta-Reise vom 16.08. bis 30.08.1983 Reise-Nr. 54532

Sehr geehrte Herren,

am 14. Juli buchte ich bei Ihnen für mich und meine Mutter vom 16. August bis 30. August 1983 eine zweiwöchige Flugpauschalreise nach Kreta mit Unterkunft und Vollpension. Leider muß ich Ihnen mitteilen, daß wir mit der Reise recht unzufrieden waren und zwar aus folgenden Gründen:

1. Beim Bustransfer vom Flughafen zum Hotel ist unser Reisekoffer verlorengegangen. Daher mußten wir Ersatzkleidung beschaffen. Mein Rechtsanwalt hat mich darauf aufmerksam gemacht, daß Sie als Reiseveranstalter dafür haften müssen, und nicht die Fluggesellschaft und das Busunternehmen, wie der Reiseleiter am Urlaubsort behauptete.
2. Die Betten in unseren Hotelzimmern wurden nie gemacht.
3. Die Zimmer wurden nicht gereinigt.
4. Das Essen war zwar nicht schlecht, aber die Portionen waren immer recht klein—Kinderportionen würde ich sagen.
5. Der Fahrstuhl war häufig außer Betrieb und unsere Zimmer lagen im 5. Stock.

Bereits am Urlaubsort habe ich mich bei unserem Reiseleiter beschwert. Er hat uns lediglich an die Hotelleitung verwiesen.

Ich verlange nun von Ihnen zumindest einen Teil des Reisepreises als Schadenersatz zurück. Andernfalls werde ich die Angelegenheit meinem Rechtsanwalt in Hamburg übergeben.

Hochachtungsvoll

Max Schaefer

---

der Betreff reference
Kreta–Reise or **Kretareise** visit to Crete
die Pauschalreise package holiday
unzufrieden dissatisfied
der Grund reason
der Ersatz replacement
beschaffen to get
der Rechtsanwalt solicitor
der Veranstalter organiser
das Unternehmen company
haften für to be held responsible for
behaupten to claim
außer Betrieb out of order
sich beschweren to complain
lediglich merely
verweisen to refer (someone) (to)
der Schadenersatz compensation
andernfalls otherwise
die Angelegenheit matter
übergeben hand over

Übungen

A. Answer the following questions in English:

1 Where did Max Schaefer and his mother spend their holidays?
2 To whom has Herr Schaefer written this letter and why?
3 What did he and his mother discover when they arrived at their hotel?
4 What did the courier say when they informed him about this?
5 What does Herr Schaefer say about the hotel? Give full details.
6 What is he demanding from the tour operator now?
7 What is he going to do if his demands are not met?

B. Beantworten Sie folgende Fragen:

1 Wohin fuhr Herr Schaefer im August?
2 Mit wem?
3 In was für einem Hotel haben sie gewohnt?
4 Was geschah beim Bustransfer vom Flughafen zum Hotel?
5 Was sagte der Reiseleiter dazu?
6 Warum waren Herr Schaefer und seine Mutter mit den Mahlzeiten unzufrieden?
7 Was mußten sie machen, wenn der Fahrstuhl außer Betrieb war?
8 Was hat der Reiseleiter gemacht, als sie sich bei ihm beschwerten?

C. Imagine you are Herr Max Schaefer and answer the following questions in German:

1 Wie lange waren Sie in Griechenland?
2 Auf welcher Insel waren Sie?
3 Wie sind Sie dahin gefahren?
4 Wer hat Sie begleitet?
5 Wo haben Sie dort gewohnt?
6 Wie sind Sie vom Flughafen zum Hotel gefahren?
7 Warum waren Sie mit Ihren Zimmern unzufrieden?
8 Wo haben Sie immer zu Mittag gegessen?
9 Wo haben Sie meistens zu Abend gegessen?
10 Was wollen Sie machen, falls Sie keinen Schadenersatz vom Reiseveranstalter bekommen?

D. Translate the following letter to Fernsehhaus Müller, Georg-Straße 33, Hannover 1 (Postleitzahl 3000) into German. Refer to Herr Schaefer's letter to Atlas-Reisen, the notes in the margins and the words and expressions in Section E to find the vocabulary you require. Begin your letter with *Leider*.

Heinrich Schroeder
Hamburger Allee 22
3000 Hannover 1

3rd March, 1983

[Addressee]

Dear Sir,

I regret to inform you that the colour television set (a Bravo) bought from you at the beginning of this year is no longer functioning perfectly. There is often no sound although I have seldom used the set. As the guarantee on it has not yet run out I should be grateful if you would send somebody round to put the set in order again.

Please telephone me to make an appointment. My telephone number at home is 62 64 30. Somebody is always at home during the day.

Thank you in advance for obliging me.

Yours faithfully,

Heinrich Schroeder

E.   Make sure you learn the following words and expressions:

ablaufen to run out, expire
andernfalls otherwise
die Angelegenheit the matter, affair, issue
jn auf etwas aufmerksam machen to draw someone's attention to something
ich möchte Sie darauf aufmerksam machen, daß ... I would like to draw your attention to the fact that ...
ausdrücklich verlangen to ask for specifically
außer Betrieb sein to be out of order
ausfallen to go dead, pack in (e.g. radio or TV sound)
die Bedienung service
behaupten to claim, maintain
benutzen to use
beschaffen to get, procure
sich beschweren bei to complain to
der Betreff (abbr: Betr.) reference (abbr: Ref.)
buchen to book
das Busunternehmen bus company, firm

einwandfrei perfectly, properly, faultlessly
der Ersatz replacement, substitute
der Fahrstuhl lift, elevator
der Flughafen airport
die Fluggesellschaft airline
die Flugpauschalreise air package holiday
funktionieren to function
das Gerät set, appliance
der Geschäftsleiter manager
Griechenland Greece
der Grund reason
haften für to be (held) responsible for, be liable for
die Kleidung clothes
Kreta Crete
lediglich merely
die Marke brand, brand name
in Ordnung bringen to put right
die Pauschalreise package holiday
das Personal personnel, staff
der Rechtsanwalt solicitor, lawyer
reinigen to clean

das Reisebüro travel agency (note: the name of the travel agency either follows the word Reisebüro or precedes it. In the latter case a hyphen is usually used, e.g.: Alpino-Reisebüro).

der Reiseleiter courier

der Schadenersatz compensation, damages

der Stock (das Stockwerk) floor, storey

der Tanzsaal dance hall

der Termin appointment

einen Termin vereinbaren to make an appointment, fix a day

die Unterkunft accommodation

unzufrieden sein to be dissatisfied

ich war mit dem Hotel recht unzufrieden I was very dissatisfied with the hotel/the hotel did not come up to my expectations

vereinbaren to arrange, agree upon (e.g. make an appointment)

verweisen an (+ acc.) to refer to, direct to

F. Imagine you have just returned home from your holiday in Spain. Write a letter of complaint to the travel agency Alpino-Reisebüro, Gartenstraße 20, Tübingen (Postleitzahl 7400), where you booked your holiday and draw the attention of the manager (Geschäftsleiter) to the fact that the Hotel you stayed at in Torremolinos (Hotel Cleopatra) did not come up to your expectations because the service was bad and the staff impolite. There was also no colour television set in your room, though you had specifically asked for one when booking the room. The music in the dance hall was so loud at night that you found it difficult to sleep. You will find all the words and expressions you require in this unit.

Arbeitssuche

Claire Baggley
16 Seaton Road
Seaton
Cumbria CA14 1DT
England

Seaton, den 30.4.83

Arbeitsamt
Wolbecker Straße 45

D-4400 Münster

Betreff: Arbeitssuche

Ich bin eine achtzehnjährige englische Studentin und studiere zur Zeit in Manchester. Dieses Jahr möchte ich meine Sommerferien in der Bundesrepublik verbringen, um meine Deutschkenntnisse zu erweitern. Deshalb suche ich eine Arbeitsstelle in Münster und Umgebung, entweder in einem Hotel oder in einer Fabrik, wo ich mit Deutschen arbeiten könnte. In den letzten Sommerferien war ich in einem englischen Warenhaus beschäftigt und z.Zt. arbeite ich hin und wieder als Kellnerin in einem großen Hotel in Manchester, um nebenbei etwas Geld zu verdienen.

Ich könnte am 15. Juli anfangen und möchte bis zum 30. August in Deutschland bleiben. Für eine Halbtagsbeschäftigung würde ich mich auch interessieren. Teilen Sie mir bitte mit, ob Sie für mich eine passende Arbeit haben, und wenn nicht, ob Sie eine geeignete Stellung vermitteln könnten. Ich wäre Ihnen dafür sehr dankbar. Fotokopien meiner Zeugnisse in Maschinenschreiben und Deutsch lege ich Ihnen bei.

Wenn Sie nichts Passendes für mich haben, würde ich mich sehr freuen, wenn Sie mir Namen von Arbeitgebern in Münster übermitteln könnten, die in den Sommerferien ausländische Studenten beschäftigen.

Mit freundlichen Grüßen

Claire Baggley

Anlagen
2 Zeugnisabschriften

zur Zeit (z.Zt.)	at present
verbringen	to spend (time)
erweitern	improve
die Umgebung	surroundings
beschäftigt	employed
nebenbei	on the side
eine Halbtagsbeschäftigung	part-time job
passend	suitable
geeignet	suitable
vermitteln	to arrange
der Arbeitgeber	employer
übermitteln	to convey
die Anlage	enclosure
das Zeugnis	certificate
die Abschrift	copy

Übungen

A. Answer the following questions in English:

1 Where does Claire want to spend her holidays and why?
2 What kind of work is she looking for?
3 Where was she employed during her last summer vacation?
4 What does she do to earn some extra money during term time?
5 Why has she written this letter to the Employment Exchange Office (Job Centre) in Münster?
6 What has she enclosed with her letter?
7 What has she asked the Employment Exchange Office to do if no suitable work is available for her?
8 Why does she want to work with Germans?

B. Beantworten Sie folgende Fragen:

1 Was ist Claire von Beruf?
2 Warum möchte sie in den Sommerferien nach Deutschland fahren?
3 Was für Arbeit sucht sie?
4 Wie lange möchte sie in der Bundesrepublik bleiben?
5 Was hat das Arbeitsamt in Münster von ihr erhalten?
6 Was soll das Arbeitsamt ihr schicken, wenn es keine passende Arbeitsstelle für sie gibt?
7 Warum arbeiten so viele Studenten in den Sommerferien?

C. Imagine you are Claire and answer the following questions in German:

1 Wie alt sind Sie?
2 Wo studieren Sie?
3 Warum möchten Sie mit Deutschen arbeiten?
4 Wie ist das Hotel, in dem Sie manchmal als Kellnerin arbeiten?
5 Wann möchten Sie nach England zurückfahren?
6 Was für Fotokopien haben Sie Ihrem Brief an das Arbeitsamt in Münster beigelegt?
7 Bei wem haben Sie voriges Jahr in den Sommerferien gearbeitet?
8 Wozu geht man zum Arbeitsamt?

D. Complete the following letter by filling in the blanks with the information supplied in English after the blanks. Each blank must be filled in by one German word. Refer to Claire's letter to the Arbeitsamt in Münster, the notes in the margin and the words and expressions in Section E to find the vocabulary you require.

Sehr geehrte Frau Kühl!

– – (Our neighbour) Frau Metcalf hat – – – – (gave me your name) – –, (and said) daß Sie mich vielleicht – – – (during the summer holidays) – – (could put up).

– – – – – (I am sixteen years old) und besuche – – – (the local comprehensive school). Seit – – (five years) – – – (I have been learning German) aber – – (I find) – – (the language) – – (very difficult). – – –, (My mother says) Fremdsprachen – – – (are very important) für das heutige Leben. Daher – – (I would like) – – – – – –, (to spend a few weeks in Germany) – – – – – (in order to improve my knowledge of German). – – –, (Mrs Metcalf said) – – – –, (you have two daughters) – – – – – – –, (who are about as old as I am) und daß – – – – – – (they are learning English at school). – – (My parents) – – – (are very interested) – – – (in an exchange programme for pupils) – – – –, (and have requested me) – – –, (to ask you) – – – – – – – – (whether you could put me up in the summer holidays). – – – –, (My parents are willing) – – (next year) – – – (both your daughters) aufzunehmen.

Wenn es – –, (is not possible) schreiben Sie mir bitte, – – – – –, (whether you know a family) – – – – – – – – – – (that is interested in an exchange between German and English schoolgirls).

Mit freundlichen Grüßen

Jacqueline Benison

E. Make sure you learn the following words and expressions:

die Abschrift copy
die Anlage enclosure
die Arbeitsstelle job
aufnehmen to put up, accommodate
der Austausch exchange
das Austauschprogramm exchange programme
die Arbeitssuche search for work, looking for a job
beilegen to enclose
bereit sein to be prepared (to do something)
bitten to request
beschäftigen to employ, engage
die Beschäftigung job, occupation
bezahlen to pay (e.g. salary, wages, bill)

die Deutschkenntnisse (pl.) knowledge of German
erweitern to broaden, extend (one's knowledge)
die Fabrik factory
die Fotokopie photo-copy
fotokopieren to photocopy
die Fremdsprache foreign language
geeignet sein für ... to be suitable for ...
die Gesamtschule comprehensive school
die Halbtagsbeschäftigung part-time job
das heutige Leben life today
hiesig local
hin und wieder now and then

kaum hardly, scarcely	**übermitteln** to send (information), communicate, convey
kennen to know	
das Maschinenschreiben typewriting	**verbessern** to improve
die Möglichkeit possibility, opportunity	**verbringen** to spend (time)
	verdienen to earn
nebenbei on the side	**vermitteln** to arrange
ein paar a few	**vertiefen** to improve, extend (one's knowledge)
passend suitable	
der Schüleraustausch exchange programme for pupils	**das Warenhaus (das Kaufhaus)** department store
sich interessieren für be interested in	**zur Zeit (z.Zt)** at present
die Stellung job, position	**das Zeugnis** certificate

F. Write a letter to the Königshof Hotel in Bonn (Postleitzahl 5300), Adenauerallee 9–11, saying that you have heard from the Arbeitsamt in Bonn that the hotel employs students in the summer vacation. Say you would like to work there for four weeks to improve your German and ask whether you could live in the hotel if you get a job. Give them the dates that would suit you.

Stock phrases

1 Beginning a letter

Thank you very much for your letter. ⎫
Many thanks for your letter. ⎬ Vielen Dank für Deinen Brief.

I received your letter this morning. Heute morgen erhielt ich Deinen Brief.

Thank you for your letter of 14th February, 1985 (*formal*). Wir danken Ihnen für Ihr Schreiben vom 14. Februar 1985.

We acknowledge receipt of your letter of 17th April, 85 (*formal*). Wir bestätigen den Eingang Ihres Schreibens vom 17. April 85 (17.4.85).

Please excuse me for not writing earlier. Bitte entschuldige, daß ich Dir nicht früher geschrieben habe.

I have not heard from you for a long time. Seit langem habe ich nichts von Dir gehört.

We have not heard from each other for a long time. Wir haben lange nicht mehr voneinander gehört.

At last I can get down to writing to you. Endlich komme ich dazu, Dir zu schreiben.

I would like to thank you for ... Ich möchte Dir für ... danken.

I would like to inform you that ... Ich möchte Dir mitteilen, daß ...

Well, how are you? Na, wie geht es Dir?

2 General Topics

a Health and welfare

How are you? Wie geht es Dir jetzt?

How is your brother? Wie geht es Deinem Bruder?

I hope you are better. Ich hoffe, es geht Dir besser.

We do hope you recover soon. Wir hoffen sehr, Du erholst Dich bald.

I hope you get well soon. Ich wünsche Dir gute Besserung.

I wish you a speedy recovery. Ich wünsche Dir eine rasche Genesung.

I do hope you are soon up and about again. Hoffentlich bist Du bald wieder wohlauf.

I am sorry to hear that your father is in hospital. Es tut mir leid zu hören, daß Dein Vater zur Zeit im Krankenhaus liegt.

What is the matter with him? Was fehlt ihm?

I do hope the operation was a success. Hoffentlich war die Operation ein Erfolg.

I am well. Es geht mir gut.

I have a cold. ⎧ Ich bin erkältet.
⎨ Ich habe eine Erkältung.

I have caught a cold again. Ich habe mich wieder erkältet.

I have had 'flu Ich habe die Grippe gehabt.

I am not very well. Gesundheitlich geht es mir nicht sehr gut.

I'm not in very good shape. Ich bin nicht auf der Höhe.

I'm as fit as a fiddle. Ich bin kerngesund.

I don't feel too well. Ich fühle mich nicht wohl.

I am feeling much better. Ich fühle mich viel besser.

I couldn't be better. Es könnte mir nicht besser gehen.

b Moods and feelings

I am in a good/bad mood today. Ich bin heute gut/schlecht gelaunt.

I am very pleased about it.	Ich freue mich sehr darüber.
I am looking forward to it.	Ich freue mich darauf.
We are delighted about it.	Es freut uns.
We are overjoyed, of course.	Wir sind natürlich überglücklich.
We are tired but happy.	Wir sind müde doch glücklich.
That is very annoying.	Das ist sehr ärgerlich.
Please don't be cross with me.	Bitte sei mir nicht böse.
We are all very sad.	Wir sind alle sehr traurig.
I hope nothing goes wrong.	Ich hoffe, nichts geht schief.
I think it is great.	Ich finde es dufte (*or* klasse/toll/prima).
I enjoy doing it.	Es macht mir Spaß.
It is a pleasure for me.	Es ist mir ein Vergnügen.
I have been lucky again.	Ich habe nochmal Glück gehabt.
He is a lucky person.	Er ist ein Glückspilz.
I have been unlucky.	Ich habe Pech gehabt.
She is a very unlucky person.	Sie ist ein Pechvogel.
She is feeling very depressed.	Sie ist ganz deprimiert.
I am feeling miserable.	Ich bin todunglücklich.
You can't have everything.	Man kann nicht alles haben.
What a shame!	Wie schade!

c The weather

The weather is frightful (terrible/wonderful/marvellous)	Das Wetter ist zur Zeit furchtbar (schrecklich/wunderbar/herrlich).
What kind of weather have you had?	Wie war das Wetter bei Euch?
It was cold (bitterly cold/cool/warm/hot/fine/sunny/cloudy).	Es war kalt (bitterkalt/kühl/warm/heiß/heiter/sonnig/bewölkt).
It is snowing again.	Es schneit wieder.
The sun is out again.	Die Sonne läßt sich wieder blicken.
It is pouring with rain.	Es gießt in Strömen.
It is raining cats and dogs.	Es regnet Bindfäden.
We have had a wonderful summer.	Wir haben einen wunderschönen Sommer gehabt.
It has been a lovely autumn.	Es war ein wunderschöner Herbst.
What was winter like?	Wie war der Winter?
We have had a severe (mild) winter.	Wir haben einen harten (milden) Winter hinter uns.
At last spring is here.	Endlich ist der Frühling da.

d Examinations

My exams begin next month.	Meine Prüfung beginnt im nächsten Monat.
I am taking my final exams in June.	Im Juni mache ich meine Abschlußprüfung.
We wish you the best of luck in the examination.	Wir wünschen Dir viel Erfolg in der Prüfung (*or* im Examen).
I have passed my exams.	Ich habe meine Prüfung bestanden.
I have done well in my exams.	Ich habe meine Prüfung gut bestanden.
I have not passed the exam.	Ich habe die Prüfung nicht bestanden.
I have failed the examination.	Ich bin in der Prüfung durchgefallen.
Hearty congratulations on your success in the examination.	Herzliche Glückwünsche zum Erfolg in der Prüfung.
I am sorry to hear that you have not passed the exam.	Es tut mir leid zu hören, daß Du die Prüfung nicht bestanden hast.
You shouldn't give up hope.	Du darfst die Hoffnung nicht aufgeben.

Next time things will definitely work out.	Das nächste Mal klappt es bestimmt.
I am convinced that you will manage it next time.	Ich bin überzeugt, daß Du es das nächste Mal schaffst.

3 Birth, engagement, marriage

Werner, our second son, was born on 10th February at 7.50 p.m.	Werner, unser zweiter Sohn, wurde am 10. Februar um 19.50 Uhr geboren.
It gives me great pleasure to inform you that our second daughter, Hilary, was born on 4th September at 1.12 a.m.	Mit großer Freude teile ich Euch mit, daß unsere zweite Tochter, Hilary, am 4. September um 01.12 Uhr das Licht der Welt erblickt hat.
Both mother and child are well.	Mutter und Kind sind wohlauf.
I have got engaged to Karl.	Ich habe mich mit Karl verlobt.
Jutta and I have got engaged.	Jutta und ich haben uns verlobt.
We are getting married on 22nd June.	Wir heiraten am 22. Juni.
Karl and I have got married.	Karl und ich haben geheiratet.
The registry office marriage ceremony (church marriage ceremony) will take place on Saturday, 25th February.	Die standesamtliche Trauung (kirchliche Trauung) findet am Sonnabend, dem 25. Februar statt.
The wedding is taking place on Saturday, 25th February.	Die Hochzeit findet am Samstag, dem 25. Februar statt.
I would like to congratulate you on the birth of your baby son.	Ich gratuliere Euch herzlichst zur Geburt Eures Sohnes.
My warmest congratulations on your engagement to Jutta.	Ich gratuliere Dir herzlichst zu Deiner Verlobung mit Jutta.
I would like to congratulate you both on your engagement.	Ich gratuliere Euch herzlichst zu Eurer Verlobung.
Hearty congratulations on your marriage.	Herzliche Glückwünsche zur Hochzeit.
I wish both of you happiness and success.	Ich wünsche Euch beiden viel Glück und Erfolg.
All the best for the future.	Alles Gute für die Zukunft.

4 Bereavement and condolences

I wish to inform you that my father died on Friday, 16th May.	Ich muß Dir mitteilen, daß mein Vater am Freitag, dem 16. Mai gestorben ist.
I am sorry to have to tell you that my mother died in hospital on Saturday, 19th January.	Leider muß ich Dir mitteilen, daß meine Mutter am Donnerstag, dem 19. Januar im Krankenhaus gestorben ist.
The funeral will take place on Monday, 21st January.	Die Trauerfeier findet am Montag, dem 21. Januar statt.
The funeral took place last Tuesday.	Die Trauerfeier fand am vorigen Dienstag statt.
The funeral was attended only by close relatives.	Die Trauerfeier fand im engsten Familienkreis statt.
The news of your father's death was a great shock to me.	Die Nachricht vom Tod Deines Vaters hat mich tief erschüttert.
I was sorry to hear of the death of your mother.	Mit großer Trauer habe ich vom Tod Deiner Mutter gehört.
My thoughts will be with all of you on Saturday.	In Gedanken werde ich am Samstag bei Euch allen sein.
Our family life revolved around him.	Er war der Mittelpunkt unserer Familie.

I always looked up to her.

Sie war für mich persönlich immer ein großes Vorbild.

Her death is a great loss for us.

Ihr Tod ist ein großer Verlust für uns.

Once again, many thanks for your sympathy.

Nochmals, vielen Dank für Deine Anteilnahme.

5 Christmas, New Year and birthdays

a Greetings

Happy Birthday

Many happy returns of the day ⎫

Herzliche Glückwünsche zum Geburtstag.

All the best for the coming year.
(Birthday greeting)

Alles Gute für das neue Lebensjahr.

I'd like to wish you a very happy birthday.

Ich gratuliere Dir recht herzlich zum Geburtstag.

I wish you a merry Christmas and all the best for the New Year.

Ich wünsche Dir ein frohes Weihnachtsfest und alles Gute zum Jahreswechsel.

A merry Christmas and a happy New Year.

Fröhliche Weihnachten und ein glückliches Neues Jahr.

I wish you good health and happiness in the New Year.

Ich wünsche Dir ein gesundes und glückliches Neues Jahr.

I wish you a happy New Year.

Ich wünsche Dir einen guten Rutsch ins Neue Jahr.

All the best for the New Year.

Alles Gute fürs Neue Jahr!

b Giving and receiving presents

I wanted to give you a small present.

Ich wollte Dir eine Kleinigkeit schenken.

I wanted to give you a little treat.

Ich wollte Dir eine kleine Freude machen.

I do hope you like it!

Hoffentlich gefällt es Dir!

Many thanks for the lovely present.

Herzlichen Dank für das schöne Geschenk.

I would like to thank you very much for the lovely ...

Ich bedanke mich recht herzlich für das tolle ...

   birthday present

   Geburtstagsgeschenk

   Christmas present

   Weihnachtsgeschenk

   wedding present

   Hochzeitsgeschenk

I am writing at once to thank you for sending me such a wonderful present.

Ich muß gleich schreiben, Dir für das wunderschöne Geschenk zu danken.

It was very kind of you to think of me.

Es war sehr freundlich von Dir, an mich zu denken.

It was awfully nice of you to send me such an expensive present.

Es war furchtbar nett von Dir, mir ein so teures Geschenk zu schicken.

I like the present very much.

Das Geschenk gefällt mir sehr.

6 Invitations and responses

Would you like to visit us in the summer holidays?

Has Du Lust, uns in den Sommerferien zu besuchen?

We would like to invite you to spend Christmas with us.

Wir möchten Dich einladen, Weihnachten bei uns zu verbringen.

We should be very pleased if you could come.

Wir würden uns freuen, wenn Du kommen könntest.

I should be very pleased if you could visit me next year.	Es würde mich sehr freuen, wenn Du mich im nächsten Jahr besuchen könntest.
Would you care to visit me at Easter?	Hättest Du Lust, mich zu Ostern zu besuchen?
I would like to thank you for your kind invitation to visit you in August.	Ich danke Dir sehr für Deine freundliche Einladung, Dich im August zu besuchen.
Many thanks for your invitation to attend Jutta's and Karl's wedding.	Herzlichen Dank für die Einladung zu Juttas und Karls Hochzeit.
I should be delighted to come.	Ich komme sehr gern.
Unfortunately I must postpone the visit.	Leider muß ich meinen Besuch verschieben.
Would it be possible to postpone the visit?	Wäre es möglich, den Besuch zu verschieben?
I am very sorry but I won't be able to come.	Es tut mir sehr leid, aber ich kann nicht kommen.
I very much regret that I won't be able to come (formal).	Ich bedauere es sehr, daß ich nicht kommen kann.
Unfortunately this is not possible as we have a visitor (visitors) at that time.	Leider geht es nicht, da wir zu dieser Zeit Besuch bekommen.
We won't be able to come after all as my mother is in hospital.	Wir werden nun doch nicht kommen können, denn meine Mutter liegt zur Zeit im Krankenhaus.

7 Holidays

a Making plans

I am on holiday from 23rd June until 4th July.	Ich habe vom 23. Juni bis zum 4. Juli Ferien.
We are going away on holiday on 16th June.	Wir fahren am 16. Juni in Urlaub.
We are going to France at the beginning of/in the middle of/at the end of July.	Wir fahren Anfang Juli/Mitte Juli/Ende Juli nach Frankreich.
This year we were in Switzerland for a fortnight.	Dieses Jahr waren wir zwei Wochen lang in der Schweiz.
We are spending our winter holiday in Austria.	Wir verbringen unseren Winterurlaub in Österreich.
We want to go skiing and ice-skating there.	Wir wollen dort Ski und Schlittschuh laufen.
We are travelling back on 28th December.	Wir fahren am 28. Dezember zurück.
We are returning home on 15th May.	Wir kehren am 15. Mai nach Hause zurück.
We won't be returning home until 30th October.	Wir fahren erst am 30. Oktober nach Hause zurück.

b Booking ahead

Please send me brochures about holidays and holiday activities in Baden-Baden.	Bitte schicken Sie mir Prospekte über Ferien und Freizeitmöglichkeiten in Baden-Baden.
Please send me a hotel guide as soon as possible.	Bitte schicken Sie mir umgehend einen Hotelführer.
We require accommodation for two adults and two children aged four and three.	Wir brauchen Unterkunft für zwei Erwachsene und zwei Kinder im Alter von vier und drei Jahren.

I am interested in:
    private lodgings
    holiday flats
    a guest-house
    a hotel
    an inn
    a farmhouse
We would like to spend our holidays in your
establishment.
Please let me know your terms for bed and
breakfast, half board and full board.

Please let me have your terms as soon as
possible.
Please let me know whether you require a
deposit.
Please find enclosed an international postal
reply coupon.
We would appreciate it if you would let us
know soon whether we can stay at your
establishment or not.
I would like to reserve two single rooms
from 15th April to 25th April, 1985.

I would like to reserve a double room with
an extra bed.
Please reserve a double room for us with:

    breakfast
    half board
    full board
    running cold and hot water

    a shower
    a bath
We require two double rooms at around
DM50.00 per room per night.
The room should not cost more than
DM40.00 per night.
We require room for a caravan (a tent) from
15th July until 30th July.

Has the campsite got:
    electricity?
    toilets?
    shower rooms?
    washrooms?
    a food shop?
Please let me know what facilities the
campsite offers.
We would like to book two beds in your
youth hostel for 26th and 27th August.

Would you please cancel the reservation I

Ich interessiere mich für:
    Privatzimmer
    Ferienwohnungen
    ein Gasthaus/eine Pension
    ein Hotel
    einen Gasthof
    einen Bauernhof
Wir möchten unsere Ferien in Ihrem
    Haus verbringen.
Bitte teilen Sie mir Ihre Bedingungen für
    Übernachtung mit Frühstück sowie für
    Halb- und Vollpension mit.
Bitte teilen Sie mir Ihre Bedingungen so
    bald wie möglich mit.
Bitte schreiben Sie mir, ob Sie eine
    Anzahlung verlangen.
Anbei finden Sie einen internationalen
    Postantwortschein.
Es wäre nett, wenn Sie uns bald mitteilen
    könnten, ob wir bei Ihnen übernachten
    können.
Hiermit möchte ich zwei Einzelzimmer
    für die Zeit vom 15. April bis zum
    25. April 1985 reservieren.
Ich möchte ein Doppelzimmer mit
    einem Zustellbett bestellen.
Reservieren Sie bitte für uns ein
    Doppelzimmer mit
    Frühstück
    Halbpension
    Vollpension
    fließendem kaltem und warmem
        Wasser
    Dusche
    Bad
Wir brauchen zwei Doppelzimmer um
    DM50,– pro Zimmer und Übernachtung.
Das Zimmer darf nicht mehr als DM40,–
    pro Übernachtung kosten.
Wir brauchen Platz für einen
    Wohnwagen (ein Zelt) für die Zeit vom
    15. Juli bis zum 30. Juli.
Hat der Campingplatz
    Strom?
    Toiletten?
    Duschräume?
    Waschräume?
    ein Lebensmittelgeschäft?
Teilen Sie mir bitte mit, welche
    Einrichtungen der Campingplatz bietet.
Wir möchten zwei Betten für den
    26. und 27. August in Ihrer
    Jugendherberge reservieren.
Würden Sie bitte meine Reservierung

made for the 26th and 27th August.

c Finding the way and giving directions

What is the best way of getting to your house?

How long does it take to get there?

Where have I got to change (trains etc)?
Do I have to change anywhere?
Where shall we meet?
You have to change in Hamburg.
The best thing is to take a taxi.
Then you take the Underground.
You get out at the third station/the third stop.
Take the second street on the right.
I shall pick you up.
I'll pick you up at the airport.
I'll wait for you at the bus stop.
After that you have to take a No. 34 bus.

You have to walk to the nearest underground station.
It is not far to walk.
You will be here in ten minutes.
Ring me from the airport.
I'll ring you as soon as I arrive.

d Lost property

I think I left the umbrella in my hotel room.

If I am not mistaken I had room 132.

I am sure that I forgot my wallet in your bank.
I left my briefcase containing my passport and important documents on the express train D-796 Stuttgart–Bremerhaven on 18th June, 1984.
Has somebody handed in the handbag at your Lost Property Office?
Has the travelling-bag been handed in at your office?
Would you please send me the parcel to the address above.
Would you please be kind enough to send me the parcel by special delivery.

Of course I will refund the postage and packing costs.

e On return

We had a fantastic time.
This place is simply terrific.
We had lots of fun.

---

für den 26. und 27. August streichen.

Wie kommt man am besten zu Dir?

Wie lange braucht man, dahin zu kommen?
Wo muß ich umsteigen?
Muß ich irgendwo umsteigen?
Wo wollen wir uns treffen?
Du mußt in Hamburg umsteigen.
Am besten fährst Du mit einem Taxi.
Du mußt mit der U-Bahn weiterfahren.
Du mußt an der dritten Station/ Haltestelle aussteigen.
Nimm die zweite Straße rechts.
Ich werde Dich abholen.
Ich hole Dich vom Flughafen ab.
Ich warte auf Dich an der Bushaltestelle.
Du mußt mit der Buslinie 34 weiterfahren.

Du mußt zu Fuß zur nächsten U-Bahnstation laufen.
Es ist nicht weit zu Fuß.
In zehn Minuten bist Du bei uns.
Ruf mich vom Flughafen an.
Nach meiner Ankunft werde ich Dich sofort anrufen.

Ich glaube, ich habe den Regenschirm in meinem Hotelzimmer liegenlassen.
Wenn ich mich nicht irre, hatte ich Zimmer 132.
Ich bin sicher, daß ich meine Brieftasche in Ihrer Bank vergessen habe.
Am 18. Juni 1984 habe ich meine Aktentasche mit meinem Reisepaß und wichtigen Dokumenten im D-Zug 796 Stuttgart–Bremerhaven liegenlassen.
Hat jemand die Handtasche in Ihrem Fundbüro abgegeben?
Ist die Reisetasche bei Ihnen abgegeben worden?
Würden Sie mir bitte das Päckchen an die obige Adresse schicken.
Würden Sie bitte so freundlich sein und mir das Päckchen durch Eilboten schicken.

Selbstverständlich werde ich Ihnen die Porto- und Verpackungskosten erstatten.

Wir haben uns großartig unterhalten.
Hier ist es einfach herrlich.
Wir haben uns köstlich amüsiert.

What was the weather like on holiday?	Wie war das Wetter im Urlaub (in den Ferien)?
I do hope you had good weather!	Hoffentlich hast Du gutes Wetter gehabt!
What was the holiday like?	Wie war der Urlaub?
What do you think of the Italian cuisine?	Was hältst Du von der italienischen Küche?
What was the food like at the holiday resort?	Wie war das Essen am Urlaubsort?
Did you put on weight this time?	Hast Du diesmal zugenommen?
Have you lost weight again?	Hast Du wieder abgenommen?

8 Letters of complaint

a Articles bought

I was very surprised at the size of your bill, which I received yesterday.	Ich war über den hohen Betrag der Rechnung, die ich gestern von Ihnen erhielt, sehr überrascht.
I regret to inform you that ...	Leider muß ich Ihnen mitteilen, daß ...
I wish to draw your attention to the fact that ...	Hiermit möchte ich Sie darauf aufmerksam machen, daß ...
I ordered two books from you on 9th January, 1985. These have still not arrived.	Am 9. Januar 1985 bestellte ich bei Ihnen zwei Bücher. Sie sind immer noch nicht eingetroffen.
I have not received the articles to date.	Bis heute habe ich die Waren nicht erhalten.
I am still waiting in vain for the delivery.	Bis heute warte ich vergeblich auf die Lieferung.
Please see to it that the parcel is here by 15th March, 1985.	Bitte sorgen Sie dafür, daß die Sendung bis zum 15.3.1985 hier eintrifft.
You have not given me a reason for the delay.	Einen Grund für die Verzögerung haben Sie mir nicht mitgeteilt.
I must hold you responsible for the damages incurred.	Ich muß Sie für den Schaden haftbar machen.
I demand compensation from you on account of the loss.	Ich verlange nun von Ihnen Schadenersatz wegen des Verlustes.
The hair-drier which I received today is damaged.	Der Fön, den ich heute erhielt, ist beschädigt.
I have hardly used the hair-drier and it is already out of order.	Ich habe den Fön kaum benutzt und er funktioniert schon nicht mehr.
I am returning the hair-drier to you and request a replacement.	Ich habe Ihnen den Fön zurückgeschickt und bitte um eine Ersatzlieferung.
I cannot understand this approach.	Ich verstehe dieses Verhalten nicht.
I am handing over the matter to my solicitor/ lawyer.	Ich habe die Angelegenheit meinem Rechtsanwalt übergeben.

b Holidays

There was no running hot and cold water in our room.	Es gab kein fließendes warmes und kaltes Wasser in unserem Zimmer.
I was highly dissatisfied with the service.	Ich war mit der Bedienung recht unzufrieden.
The hotel staff was very impolite.	Das Hotelpersonal war sehr unhöflich.
The rooms were dirty and the beds were not made.	Die Zimmer waren schmutzig und die Betten wurden nicht gemacht.
The lifts were often out of order.	Die Fahrstühle waren häufig außer Betrieb.
The food was not good and the portions were very small.	Das Essen schmeckte nicht und die Portionen waren sehr klein.

One of the taps in our room was dripping all the time.	Einer der Wasserhähne in unserem Zimmer tropfte die ganze Zeit.
It was noisy at night and we found it difficult to get to sleep.	Nachts gab es immer so viel Lärm, daß wir schlecht einschlafen konnten.
We did not have a room facing the sea, as promised.	Obwohl zugesagt, hatten wir kein Zimmer auf der Meeresseite.
The hotel was fully booked and we were put up in a small guest-house in the town's main street.	Das Hotel war belegt und wir wurden in einem kleinen Gasthaus in der Hauptverkehrsstraße untergebracht.
The plane was late and we missed our connection.	Das Flugzeug hatte Verspätung und wir haben unseren Anschluß verpaßt.
The courier did not do anything about it.	Der Reiseleiter hat nichts unternommen.

9 Looking for a job or a language course

I would like to apply for the post of secretary which was advertised in the "Frankfurter Rundschau" today.	Ich möchte mich um die Stellung als Sekretärin bewerben, die heute in der „Frankfurter Rundschau" ausgeschrieben war.
Please let me know if you can offer me a job.	Bitte teilen Sie mir mit, ob Sie mir eine Arbeitsstelle vermitteln können.
I would be pleased if I could have a job with you in the summer holidays.	Ich würde mich freuen, wenn ich in den Sommerferien bei Ihnen arbeiten könnte.
I am looking for a situation as an au pair from 2nd May, 1985 until 15th June, 1986.	Ich suche eine Au-Pair-Stellung für die Zeit vom 2. Mai 1985 bis zum 15. Juni 1986.
I am interested in a situation as an au pair in Munich.	Ich interessiere mich für eine Au-Pair-Stellung in München.
I am writing to enquire whether you know of any au pair situation in Hamburg that is available from July onwards.	Ich möchte anfragen, ob Ihnen eine Au-Pair-Stellung in Hamburg bekannt ist, die ab Juli frei wird.
I am interested in an exchange between English and German schoolchildren.	Ich interessiere mich für einen Austausch zwischen englischen und deutschen Schülern.
I am writing to enquire whether you could send me information about the possibilities of an exchange between English and German music groups.	Ich möchte anfragen, ob Sie mich über die Möglichkeit eines Austausches zwischen englischen und deutschen Musikgruppen informieren können.
I am enclosing my handwritten curriculum vitae and copies of my certificates.	Ich lege Ihnen einen handgeschriebenen Lebenslauf und Abschriften meiner Zeugnisse bei.
Please find enclosed a stamped envelope.	Anbei finden Sie einen frankierten Briefumschlag.
I would like to take part in a German course at your school in July.	Ich möchte gern im Juli an einem Deutschkurs an Ihrer Schule teilnehmen.
Please let me know the dates of your courses.	Teilen Sie mir bitte die Termine Ihrer Kurse mit.
Could you help me in finding a room?	Könnten Sie mir bei der Zimmersuche behilflich sein?

10 Placing and cancelling orders and subscriptions

I would like to order the following books:

Hiermit bestelle ich die folgenden Bücher:

I would like to order two sleeping bags.
Please let me know what is available.

Ich möchte zwei Schlafsäcke bestellen.
Bitte schreiben Sie mir, was Sie vorrätig haben.

Please send me your current catalogue.

Bitte schicken Sie mir Ihren neuesten Katalog.

I would like to subscribe to your newspaper for a year.

Ich möchte Ihre Zeitung für ein Jahr abonnieren.

I would like to subscribe to your magazine from 10.2.1985 until further notice.

Hiermit möchte ich ab 10.2.1985 bis auf weiteres Ihre Zeitschrift abonnieren.

I would like to renew my subscription to your newspaper for another year.

Ich möchte mein Abonnement auf Ihre Zeitung für ein weiteres Jahr erneuern.

I no longer wish to receive/subscribe to your magazine.

Ich möchte Ihre Zeitschrift nicht mehr beziehen/abonnieren.

I do not wish to renew my subscription to your newspaper any longer.

Ich möchte mein Abonnement Ihrer Zeitung nicht weiter erneuern.

Please cancel my order.

Ich bitte Sie, meine Bestellung zu streichen.

Please send me your invoice at your earliest convenience.

Bitte schicken Sie mir umgehend Ihre Rechnung.

Please let me have the information as soon as possible.

Bitte geben Sie mir so bald wie möglich Bescheid.

I am enclosing a cheque for £52.50.

Ich lege Ihnen einen Scheck über £52.50 bei.

I have instructed my bank to send you DM25.00.

Ich habe meine Bank angewiesen, Ihnen DM25,– zu überweisen.

I am enclosing an international postal reply coupon.

Einen internationalen Postantwortschein füge ich bei.

11 Finishing letters

a Informal

Hoping to hear from you soon.
I'll get in touch again soon.
That will be all for today.
That's all for today.
I'll close now.
Until next time!
Do write to me again soon.
I do hope you will write to me again soon.

Laß bald von Dir hören!
Ich lasse bald wieder von mir hören.
Das wär's für heute.
Das ist alles für heute.
Ich mache jetzt Schluß.
Bis zum nächsten Mal!
Schreib mir bitte bald wieder!
Hoffentlich schreibst Du mir bald wieder!

I shall expect a long letter from you next time.
Take care of yourself.
All the best to you.

Das nächste Mal erwarte ich einen langen, ausführlichen Brief von Dir.
Laß es Dir gut gehen!
Alles Gute für Dich.

Lots of love.

{ Alles Liebe
  Viele liebe Grüße
  Herzliche Grüße

Kind regards
Regards to you and your parents.

Herzliche Grüße an Dich und Deine Eltern.

My parents and I send you our love.	Meine Eltern und ich senden Dir die herzlichsten Grüße.
Yours sincerely (*familiar*).	Mit herzlichen Grüßen.
Regards from all of us.	Herzliche Grüße von uns allen.
We all send you our best wishes.	Wir alle senden Dir die besten Wünsche.
Yours sincerely (*polite or formal*)	Mit freundlichen Grüßen.
Yours affectionately	Mit vielen lieben Grüßen.
PS (postscript)	PS (Postskriptum)

b Formal

Please write to me soon to let me know whether this is possible or not.	Bitte schreiben Sie mir so bald wie möglich, ob das geht!
Please let me have the necessary information at your earliest convenience.	Bitte geben Sie mir umgehend Bescheid!
I would appreciate an early reply.	Für eine baldige Antwort wäre ich Ihnen dankbar.
Thanking you in advance for your assistance.	Ich danke Ihnen im voraus für Ihre Bemühungen.
Thanking you in advance for obliging me.	Ich danke Ihnen im voraus für Ihr Entgegenkommen.

Yours faithfully	{ Mit vorzüglicher Hochachtung (*very formal*) Hochachtungsvoll (*formal*) Mit freundlichen Grüßen (*less formal*)
Enclosures(s)	Anlage(n)

Postal terms

(der) Absender	Sender
(das) Aerogramm *or* (der) Luftpostleichtbrief	Aerogramme
Bei (*e.g.* bei Schmidt *or* b/Schmidt)	c/o = care of (e.g. c/o Schmidt)
(die) Blindensendung	No postage required (addressee blind)
(der) Briefkasten	Letter box
(die) Briefmarke	Stamp
(der) Briefträger/Briefzusteller	Postman
(die) Büchersendung	Book-post
(die) Bundespost (BP)	Postal authority of the Federal Republic of
(die) Deutsche Bundespost (DBP)	Germany (West Germany)
Dringend	Urgent
(die) Drucksache	Printed Matter
Drucksache zu ermäßigter Gebühr	Printed Matter at Reduced Rate
Eigenhändig	To be handed personally to the addressee by the postman
Eilboten/Durch Eilboten/Per Eilboten	Express Delivery or Special Delivery
(der) Eilbrief	Express Letter
(die) Eilsendung	Express Delivery Item
Eilt sehr	Very Urgent
(die) Eilzustellung	Express Delivery
(das) Einschreiben	Registered
(der) Empfänger	Recipient/Addressee
Empfänger unbekannt verzogen	Recipient has moved away without leaving an address
Empfänger verzogen	Recipient/Addressee has gone away
Falls unzustellbar, bitte (an Absender) zurück	If undelivered please return (to sender)
Falls (Empfänger) verzogen bitte (mit neuer Adresse) zurück	If addressee has moved please return to sender (with new address)
Falls verzogen bitte nachsenden	If addressee has moved please forward
frankieren/bitte frankieren freimachen/bitte freimachen	To affix stamp(s)/please affix stamp(s)
(die) Gebühr	Postage/Charge/Fee/Rate
Gebührenfrei	No postage required
Gebühr zahlt Empfänger	Postage will be paid by addressee
Internationaler Antwortschein/ Postantwortschein	International (Postal) Reply Coupon
Mit Luftpost/per Luftpost	By Air Mail
Muster ohne Wert	Sample(s) without any commercial value
Nicht frankieren	Do not affix stamps
Nicht freimachen	Do not affix stamps
Nicht knicken	Do not bend
(das) Päckchen	Small parcel
(das) Paket	Large parcel
Persönlich	Personal
(das) Porto	Postage
Portofrei	No postage required
Porto zahlt Empfänger	Postage will be paid by addressee
(das) Postamt	Post Office

(die) Postkarte	Postcard
Postlagernd	Poste Restante, to be called for
(die) Postleitzahl	Postal Code
(das) Telegramm	Telegram
Verzollt	Customs Duty Paid
Vorsicht — Glas	Glass — With Care
Vorsicht — zerbrechlich	Fragile — Handle with Care
(die) Zustellgebühr	Delivery Charge
(der) Zoll	Customs Duty
(das) Zollamt	Customs Office
Zollamtlich abgefertigt	Checked by Customs
Zollfrei	No Customs Duty Required/Free of Duty
zu Händen (z.H./z.Hd.)	For the attention of (e.g. after the name of the company on an envelope as part of the address, or on the notepaper):

Krüger & Mayer GmbH
z.H. Herrn Vogt
Uhland Straße 66

2000 Hamburg 70

Abbreviations

Abk.	Abkürzung	Abbreviation
Abs.	Absender	Sender
Abt.	Abteilung	Department (Dept.)
AG	Aktiengesellschaft	Public Limited Company (PLC)
Betr./betr.	Betreff/betreffend/betrifft	Regarding (Re:)/Reference (Ref.)
bzw.	beziehungsweise	Respectively
ca.	circa, zirka	About, approximately (ca.)
d.h.	das heißt	That is (i.e.)
d.i.	das ist	
d.J.	dieses Jahres	Of this year
d.M.	dieses Monats	Of this month
DM	Deutsche Mark	German mark(s)
evtl.	eventuell	Possibly, possible
Fa.	Firma	Firm or Messrs.
Fam.	Familie	Family
Gebr.	Gebrüder	Brothers (Bros.)
GmbH	Gesellschaft mit beschränkter Haftung	Private Limited Company
i.A.	im Auftrag	For, on behalf of (pp.)
i.H.	im Hause	In the firm/establishment, on the premises
Inh.	Inhaber/Inhalt	Proprietor/contents
inkl.	inklusive	Including, inclusive of
KG	Kommanditgesellschaft	Limited Partnership
lt.	laut	According to
MWSt/MwSt	Mehrwertsteuer	Value Added Tax
No./Nr.	Numero/Nummer	Number
Pf.	Pfennig	Pfennig
PLZ	Postleitzahl	Post Code
s.o.	siehe oben	See above
s.u.	siehe unten	See below
Str.	Straße	Street, road
u.	und	And
u.a.	unter anderem	Among other things
usf.	und so fort	And so forth
usw.	und so weiter	and so on (etc.)
z.B.	zum Beispiel	For example (e.g.)
z.H./z.Hd.	zu Händen	For the attention of
z.T.	zum Teil	Partly
z.Z./z.Zt	zur Zeit	At present, for the time being

Vocabulary

Note: In the following list all nouns ending with **-e** form their plural with **-n**. All nouns ending with **-heit**, **keit**, **schaft** and **-ung** form their plural by adding **-en**. Otherwise the plural forms of only those nouns which are useful in the context of this book are given.

Generally, where a word has several meanings only those which are applicable in this book are given.

The following abbreviations have been used:

acc. = accusative; adj. = adjective; adv. = adverb; dat. = dative; jm. = jemandem (dat.); jn. = jemanden (acc.); pl. = plural; wk. masc. = weak masculine.

abholen	to pick up, collect, call for, fetch
ablaufen	to expire, run out
der Abreisetag	day of departure
der Abschied	farewell, departure
abnehmen	to lose weight, decrease
das Album (*pl:* **Alben)**	album
allerlei	all kinds of
alles Gute	all the best
das Altenheim/ Altersheim (-e)	home for old people
andernfalls	otherwise, or else
anfahren	to run into, collide with
anfangen	to start, commence, begin
die Angelegenheit	the matter, affair, issue
der Anreisetag/ Ankunftstag	day of arrival
anrufen	to telephone, ring up
die Anschrift (-en)	address
die Ansichtskarte	picture postcard
die Anzeige	announcement, notice, advertisement
anzeigen	to announce, notify
die Arbeitsstelle	job, situation, place of work
aufhören	to cease, stop doing something

aufmerksam sein	to be courteous, kind obliging, attentive
die Aufmerksamkeit	kindness, attention
aufnehmen	to put up, accommodate
aufwachen	to wake up
ausdrücklich verlangen	to ask for specifically
außer Betrieb sein	to be out of order
ausfallen	to go dead, pack in, drop out, fail (e.g. radio or television sound), be excluded
der Ausflug (̈-e)	outing, excursion
ausführlich	in detail
aussehen	to appear, look
aussuchen	to choose, select
der Austausch	exchange
der Ausweis (-e)	identity or membership card
der Badeanzug (̈-e)	swimming costume or suit
die Badehose	swimming trunks
beabsichtigen	to intend doing, have intention
sich bedanken für (+ acc.)	to thank someone for something
bedeuten	to mean
die Bedienung	service
die Bedingung	condition
die Beerdigung	funeral, burial
sich befinden	to be located, to be found
begleiten	to accompany
behaupten	to maintain, claim
beifügen, beilegen	to enclose
bekannt	well known
bekommen	to get, receive, obtain
berühmt	famous
beschaffen	to get (hold of), procure
sich beschäftigen mit (+ dat.)	to concern or occupy oneself with
die Beschäftigung	occupation, employment
sich beschweren bei (+ dat.)	to complain to
das Besetztzeichen	engaged tone (telephone)

besitzen	to own, possess	empfangen	to receive, welcome
im Besitz sein	to be in possession (of)	empfehlen	to recommend
		der Enkel(-)	grandson, grandchild
besonders	especially, particularly	die Ente	duck
		entleihen (+ dat.)	to borrow (from)
bestehen aus (+ dat.)	to consist of	enttäuschen	to disappoint
		die Enttäuschung	disappointment
bestellen	to order, reserve	erhalten	to get, receive
der Betreff	reference	erledigen	to accomplish, finish, settle
die Bettwäsche	bedlinen		
die Beule	dent (e.g. vehicle), boil, lump, swelling (people)	erleiden	to suffer, sustain (injury, loss, etc.)
		die Ermaßigung	reduction, cut (price, tax, etc.)
bewundern	to admire		
die Bildergalerie	art gallery	der Ersatz	replacement, substitute
bildhübsch	as pretty as a picture		
brav	well-behaved	erweitern	to broaden, extend (e.g. one's knowledge)
die Brille	pair of spectacles		
buchen	to book, reserve		
die Bundesrepublik Deutschland (BRD)	Federal Republic of Germany i.e. West Germany	die Eßnische	dining alcove
		eventuell	possibly, perhaps
		fabelhaft	fabulous
die (Deutsche) Bundespost	(West German) Post Office	die Fabrik (-en)	factory
		das Fach (-er)	subject e.g. Deutsch
das Busunternehmen	bus company, firm	der Fahrlehrer	driving instructor
		die Fahrprüfung	driving test
		die Fahrschule	driving school
circa (ca.)	about, approximately	der Fahrstuhl (-er)	lift, elevator
		falls	if, in case
die Deutsche Demokratische Republik (DDR)	German Democratic Republic i.e. East Germany	der Familienkreis (-e)	family circle
		faulenzen	to be lazy, idle
die Deutschkennt- nisse (pl.)	knowledge of German	der Federball	badminton
		die Feier (-n)	celebration, party, ceremony
das Dia (-s)	slide (photograph), transparency	feiern	to celebrate
		die Ferien (pl.)	holidays
die Diele	entrance hall, vestibule	das Fest (-e)	festival, feast
		feststellen	to find out, establish, ascertain
der Dom (-e)	cathedral		
das Doppelzimmer(-)	double room	die Filiale	branch (of company etc.)
		die Firma (pl: Firmen)	company, firm
die Dusche	shower		
		fix und fertig	quite ready
das Einfamilienhaus (-er)	detached house	fliegen	to fly
		die Flitterwochen (pl.)	honeymoon
einschließlich	including, inclusive of		
einwandfrei	properly, accurately, perfectly, without trouble	der Flug (-e)	flight
		der Flughafen (-)	airport
		die Fluggesellschaft	airline
der Ehemann (-er)	husband		
der Einwohner(-)	inhabitant	die Flugpauschal- reise	air package holiday
das Einzelzimmer(-)	single room		

die Folge	result	Griechenland	Greece
der Fotoapparat (-e)	camera	großartig	great, super
		die Größe	height, size
fotokopieren	to photocopy	der Grund (-̈e)	reason
frech	cheeky	der Gruß (-̈e)	greeting, salutation
das Freibad	open-air swimming pool	gute Besserung	get well soon
		der Gutschein (-e)	voucher
sich freuen	to be pleased		
sich freuen auf (+ acc.)	to look forward to	der Hafen (-̈)	port, harbour
		haften für (+ acc.)	to be (held) responsible/liable for
sich freuen über (+ acc.)	to be pleased about		
der Friedhof (-̈e)	cemetery, graveyard	die Halbtags- beschäftigung	part-time job
fröhlich	merry, cheerful		
der Führerschein (-e)	driving licence	das Hallenbad	(indoor) swimming bath(s)
den Führerschein machen	to learn to drive, take the driving test	die Hauptsache	the main thing
		der Haufen	heap, pile
funktionieren	to function	auf einen Haufen	all together, with a rush
die Gans (-̈e)	goose	heil	safe, safely
ganz bestimmt	most definitely	heilen	to heal, cure
die Gaststätte	restaurant	die Herbergsmutter (-̈) (pl.)	youth hostel warden (female)
gefallen (+ dat.)	to like, enjoy		
es geht	it is possible, it can be done, it's working	das Herz	heart
		der Herzanfall (-̈e)	heart attack
es geht nicht	it is impossible, it can't be done, it won't do, it won't work	die Herzbeschwer- den	heart trouble, heart complaint
		herzlich	sincere, cordially, warmly
geeignet sein für (+ acc.)	to be suitable for	herzliche Grüße	kind regards
		heutzutage	nowadays
genügen	to suffice	hiesig	local
das Gerät-e	appliance, set (e.g. television set)	hiermit	herewith, hereby
		hilfsbereit	helpful
das Gepäck	baggage, luggage	hin und wieder	now and then, from time to time
Gepäck aufgeben	to send luggage in advance		
		das Hobby (-s)	hobby
das Gericht (-e)	dish, course (meal)	die Hochzeit (-en)	wedding
die Gesamtschule	comprehensive school	die Hochzeitsreise	honeymoon
		der Hochzeitstag	wedding day, anniversary
der Geschäftsleiter	manager, business manager		
		hoffen	to hope
das Gewicht	weight	hoffentlich	it is to be hoped that, hopefully
gewinnen	to win		
gewöhnlich	usually	hoffentlich geht es/ klappt es	I hope it is possible/ all right/works out
Glück haben	to be lucky		
glücklich sein	to be happy	die Hoffnung	hope
der Glückspilz	lucky person/devil	der Hotelführer	hotel guide
der Glückwunsch (-̈e)	good wishes, congratulations	das Hotelverzeichnis (-se)	list of hotels
gratulieren (+ dat.)	to congratulate		
		der Humor	(sense of) humour

immer noch	still	**laut**	loud (incl. colours!), noisy, boisterous
der Ingenieur (-e)	engineer		
die Innenstadt	town centre	**das Leben**	life
die Insel Man	Isle of Man	**lediglich**	merely, only
inzwischen	in the meantime, meanwhile	**leider**	unfortunately, I'm afraid
Italien	Italy	**leihen**	borrow, hire, lend
		das Leinen	linen
je	each	**der Leinenschlafsack (¨e)**	linen sleeping-bag
jedoch	nevertheless, however		
je mehr, desto besser	the more the better	**das Lieblingsfach (¨er)**	favourite subject
je weniger, desto besser	the less the better	**losgehen**	to set off (on foot), begin (of event)
die Jugendherberge	youth hostel	**losfahren**	to set off (using transport)
		die Lufthansa	Lufthansa (German national airline)
das Kaufhaus (¨er)	department store	**die Lust**	desire, inclination (to do something), enjoyment
kaum	hardly, scarcely		
die Kapelle	chapel		
Kärnten	Carinthia (Austrian province)	**Lust haben**	to want to/feel inclined (to do something)
kirchlich	church (adj.)		
die kirchliche Trauung	church wedding ceremony	**die Marke**	brand, trademark
klagen über (+ acc.)	to complain about	**das Maschinen-schreiben**	typewriting
die Klassenarbeit (-en)	written class test	**mehrere**	several
		die Mehrwertsteuer (MWSt.)	Value Added Tax (VAT)
klappen	to work out, be all right	**mindestens**	at least
hoffentlich ⎱	it is to be hoped that	**mitschleppen**	drag along, carry
klappt es ⎰	it will work out, I hope it works out	**mitteilen**	inform
die Kleidung	clothes, attire	**mitteleuropäische Zeit (MEZ)**	Central European Time
knuddelig	cuddly	**die Möglichkeit**	possibility, opportunity
Köln	Cologne		
der Kontakt (-e)	contact	**München**	Munich
Kontakt aufnehmen	to make contact		
die Kopfverletzung	head injury	**der Nachname (wk. masc.)**	surname
Kreta	Crete	**die Nachricht (-en)**	news
kriegen	to get, obtain		
die Kunstgalerie	art gallery	**nagelneu**	brand new
die Kunsthalle	art gallery, art museum	**näherrücken**	to draw nearer, come closer
die Küste	coast	**nebenbei**	on the side (e.g. to work on the side)
landen	to land, touch down (aeroplane)	**der Nesselschlafsack (¨e)**	cotton fabric sleeping bag
die Landung	landing		
lange/seit langem	for a long time, for ages		

das Neujahr	New Year's Day, 1st January	ruhig	quiet, calm
das neue /Neue Jahr	New Year	die Rundfahrt (-en)	round trip
nicht mehr	no longer, not any more	rüstig	active, hale and hearty
nichts Besonderes	nothing special, nothing in particular	sammeln	to collect
niedlich	cute, sweet	die Sammlung	collection
nochmals	once more, once again	der Schadenersatz	compensation, damages
normalerweise	normally, usually	der Schäferhund	Alsatian dog ("German Shepherd")
die Oper (-n)	opera	schick	smart, chic
ordnen	to arrange, sort out	schicken	to send
die Ordnung	order	schlimm	bad, sad, serious, severe
in Ordnung bringen	to put right, put in order	der Schlittschuh (-e)	skate
passen	to suit, be suitable, fit	Schlittschuh laufen (or Schlittschuh fahren)	to go (ice) skating
die Pauschalreise	package holiday		
das Pech	bad luck	die Schramme	scratch (e.g. on a vehicle)
der Pechvogel	unlucky person		
die Pension	guest house	der Schüleraustausch	exchange of pupils
das Personal	personnel, staff		
das Pflichtfach (¨er)	compulsory subject	der Schwager (¨)	brother-in-law
der Polterabend	pre-wedding party (see Unit 9, Section D).	die Schwägerin (-nen)	sister-in-law
		die Schweiz	Switzerland
der Postantwortschein (-e)	postal reply coupon	die Schwiegermutter (¨)	mother-in-law
die Postleitzahl (-en)	postal code (in figures)	selbstverständlich	of course
der Preis (-e)	prize, price	das ist selbstverständlich	that goes without saying
probieren	to try, test, check		
die Pute	turkey (hen)	sicher	sure, surely, certainly
der Puter	turkey (cock)	der Silvester	New Year's Eve
		Sizilien	Sicily
die Radtour (-en)	cycling tour	Ski laufen (or Ski fahren)	to go skiing
der Rechtsanwalt (¨e)	lawyer, solicitor		
		so etwas	something like that, such a thing
rechtzeitig	in good time, at the right time		
		sonst (or ansonsten)	otherwise
reden	to talk, speak		
reinigen	to clean		
die Reise	journey, trip	sorgen für (+ acc.)	to look after, take care of
das Reisebüro (-s)	travel agency		
der Reiseleiter	courier	sowieso	in any case, as it is
reisen	to travel	Spanien	Spain
reservieren	to reserve, book	der Spaß	fun, enjoyment
die Riviera	Riviera	es macht mir Spaß	I find it fun, I enjoy it
der Rückflug (¨e)	return flight		
die Rückkehr	return		

spätestens	at the latest	übrigens	by the way, incidentally
spazierengehen	to go for a walk, take a walk	ungefähr	about, roughly, approximately
der Spaziergang (¨e)	walk, stroll	unheimlich	very, awfully
der Stadtplan	town map	unterbringen	to accommodate, put up
der Stadtrand (¨er)	outskirts of the town or city	die Unterkunft	accommodation
der Stadtteil (-e) or Stadtviertel)	part or quarter of town or city	unzufrieden sein	to be dissatisfied
das Standesamt (¨er)	registry office	der Urlaub	holidays
standesamtliche Trauung	registry office marriage ceremony	verbessern	to improve, correct
		verbilligt	reduced in price
stattfinden	to take place	verbringen	to spend (time)
stehen (+ dat.)	suit, fit	verdienen	to earn
das Kleid steht ihr gut	the dress suits her	vereinbaren	to arrange, agree, make (e.g. appointment)
die Stellung	job, position, employment	das Vergnügen	pleasure
		der Verkehr	traffic
sterben	to die	das Verkehrsamt (¨er)	tourist information office
stets	always, regularly, constantly	die Verletzung	injury
stimmen (es stimmt)	to be correct (that is correct or right)	sich verloben	to get engaged
		der Verlobte	fiancé
der Stock	floor, storey	die Verlobte	fiancée
das Stockwerk (pl. Stockwerke)		die Verlobten	engaged couple
		die Verlobung	engagement
stolz sein auf (+ acc.)	to be proud of	der Verlust (-e)	loss
		die Vermählung	marriage, wedding
er ist stolz auf seinen Bruder	he is proud of his brother	vermitteln	to arrange (i.e. provide a service)
der Stolz	pride	verreisen	to go on a journey
der Studenten- ausweis (-e)	student identity card	verschlingen	to swallow, devour
		versuchen	to try, attempt
		vertiefen	to deepen, extend (one's knowledge of something)
tagsüber	during the day		
der Tanzsaal	dance hall	verweisen an (+ acc.)	to refer to, direct to
die Tapete (-n)	wall-paper		
tapezieren	to wallpaper	die Vollpension	full board
der Termin (-e)	appointment, date	vorbei	over, gone, past
der Tod	death	vorhaben	to have in mind, intend, plan
das Tragflügelboot (-e)	hydrofoil, jetfoil		
die Trauerfeier	funeral service	vorletzt (adj.)	last but one
die Trauung	marriage ceremony	der Vorname (wk. masc.)	first name, Christian name
Tschüß!	'Bye! (familiar)	der Vorschlag (¨e)	suggestion
die Türkei	Turkey	vorschlagen	to suggest
		sich (dat.) vorstellen	to imagine
die Überfahrt (-en)	crossing (boat)		
übergeben	to hand over	ich kann es mir (gut) vorstellen, (daß)	I can (well) imagine (that ...)
übermitteln	to convey, communicate		
übernachten	to spend the night		

das Wahlfach (¨er)	optional subject	das Wiedersehen	reunion
das Warenhaus (¨er)	department store	wiegen	to weigh
der Wasserhahn (¨e)	water-tap	wohlauf sein	to be well, in good health
die Weihnacht (Weihnachten)	Christmas	wünschen	to wish, desire
fröhliche Weihnachten	a merry Christmas	die Zeit (-en)	time, period
der Weihnachtsbaum (¨e)	Christmas tree	zur Zeit (z.Zt.)	at present, now, for the time being
das Weihnachtsfest	Christmas	der Zeitpunkt	moment, point in time
die Weihnachtskarte	Christmas card	das Zeugnis (se)	certificate
das Weihnachtslied (-er)	Christmas carol	ziemlich	rather, fairly, quite
		zunehmen	to put on weight, increase
der Weihnachtsmann	Father Christmas, Santa Claus	zurechtkommen	to manage, cope
weiterleiten an (+ acc.)	to refer (case or matter) to	zurückerstatten	to refund
		zurückfahren	to travel back, return
der Wellensittich (-e)	budgerigar	zurückkehren	to return, come back
die Welt	world	zwar	admittedly, indeed, certainly, to be sure, of course
der Wettbewerb (-e)	competition, contest	– und zwar	namely, to be precise
		das Zweifamilien-haus (¨er)	semi-detached house, house divided into two flats
		die Zwischen-landung	stopover (aeroplane)